2/93

D1212124

Weeds of Kentucky and Adjacent States

Weeds of Kentucky and Adjacent States

A Field Guide

PATRICIA DALTON HARAGAN

THE UNIVERSITY PRESS OF KENTUCKY

Text copyright © 1991 by The University Press of Kentucky,
scholarly publisher for the Commonwealth,
serving Bellarmine College, Berea College, Centre
College of Kentucky, Eastern Kentucky University,
The Filson Club, Georgetown College, Kentucky
Historical Society, Kentucky State University,
Morehead State University, Murray State University,
Northern Kentucky University, Transylvania University,
University of Kentucky, University of Louisville,
and Western Kentucky University.

Editorial and Sales Offices: Lexington, Kentucky 40508-4008

Library of Congress Cataloging-in-Publication Data

Haragan, Patricia Dalton, 1953-
    Weeds of Kentucky and adjacent states : a field guide / Patricia
Dalton Haragan.
       p. cm.
    Includes bibliographical references and indexes.
    ISBN 0-8131-1743-7 (alk. paper) :
    1. Weeds—Kentucky—Identification. I. Title.
SB612.K4H37   1991
581.6′52′09769—dc20   90-24566

This book is printed on acid-free paper meeting
the requirements of the American National Standard
for Permanence of Paper for Printed Library Materials.
⊗

This book is dedicated with reverence and love to my husband Chris and in loving memory to my mother, Margaret, and my friend, Beebee, both of whom taught me the beauty of plants.

Contents

Acknowledgments

I am deeply indebted to several people whose friendship and unfailing support have been invaluable during the time I have worked on this book. They are: Dr. James Herron, retired weed science extension specialist, University of Kentucky College of Agriculture; Dr. William Witt, Weed Science Program, University of Kentucky College of Agriculture; Drs. Carol and Jerry Baskin, School of Biological Sciences, University of Kentucky; and Dr. Mary Wharton, professor emeritus, Georgetown College. To Dr. John Thieret, I would like to give special thanks for his utmost support, guidance, patience, and expertise in reviewing the manuscript.

I wish to give special mention to the following people for their help in bringing this book to completion: Dr. Robert Ogilvie, curator of the British Columbia Provincial Museum, Victoria, for taking the time to make sure that Amy Storey's botanical illustrations were correctly drawn; Dr. Willem Meijer, School of Biological Sciences, University of Kentucky; Ms Rebecca Perry, librarian, and the staff at the Lloyd Library, Cincinnati, Ohio; Ms Tina Tillery and the staff at the University of Kentucky Seed Laboratory; and Ms Anne Kupper, secretary, University of Kentucky College of Agriculture.

To my sister, Amy Storey, go many thanks for her hard work in producing these superb illustrations. Special thanks go also to those whose financial support made this book possible: the Kentucky Foundation for Women, Inc., and the Monsanto Company. I am grateful to the New York Botanical Garden for permission to reproduce drawings from *The New Britton and Brown Third Illustrated Flora of the Northeastern United States and Adjacent Canada* by Henry A. Gleason, copyright © 1952, 1980, by the New York Botanical Garden; and to

Regina O. Hughes for permission to reproduce her drawings originally published in *Selected Weeds of the United States*, published by the U.S. Department of Agriculture in 1970.

Finally, I would like to thank all the people of the state, too numerous to mention individually, for their time and help in the field and otherwise.

Introduction

Plants respond in a variety of ways to disturbance of their habitats. Some thrive and reproduce, others die and are replaced by species better adapted to the new conditions. The plants included in this book are those that thrive in "man"-made habitats. These uncultivated plants are weeds and are defined in this guide as plants perceived to be undesirable.

Weeds have been associated with humans throughout the history of civilization. Many of the plants in our midst are not native but immigrant and, like many of our ancestors, came to the New World from Europe and Asia. As travelers have migrated from one continent to another, they have transported with them entire floras, including both weed and crop species. These plants continue to depend on human intervention for survival and have become integrated into our culture.

It follows that many of our weeds are cosmopolitan, as they are distributed throughout the state and beyond its borders. Some species are troublesome both here and in other parts of the world. For instance, common lambsquarters, common chickweed, field bindweed, and johnsongrass infest fields of vegetables, small grains, cereals, and corn both in Europe and in our region. Tropical species such as prickly sida, spurred anoda, balloonvine, and some of the amaranths have spread to Kentucky from Central and South America. In contrast, plants native to Kentucky usually have limited geographic ranges.

Weeds are of concern to us because they are abundant and costly to control. Kentucky is an agricultural state where in 1989-1990 about 5.7 million acres of field crops, including tobacco, corn, soybeans, sorghum, some small grains, and hay, were harvested. Each of these crops is associated with a weed flora that reduces its yield by competing with it and reduces its quality by contaminating the harvest. Each year over 50 million dollars are spent on weed control in corn and soybeans alone in the state. Weeds grow opportunistically also in other sites disturbed to serve human needs, such as industrial grounds, roadways, and waste places. In short, these plants have been highly successful at becoming established despite the considerable time, effort, and money spent futilely trying to eradicate them.

There is little information on how the composition of weed floras in Kentucky has changed over time. Nevertheless, a comparison of the list of weeds described in this guide with that in Dr. Harrison Garman's monograph *Some Kentucky Weeds and Poisonous Plants* (1914) reveals the appearance since the early part of this century of species new to the state. These include spurred anoda, balloonvine, palmer amaranth, eclipta, shattercane, broadleaf signalgrass, hemp sesbania, sicklepod, musk thistle, and giant foxtail. Other species previously of minor importance have become well established in the past several decades, notably witchgrass, fall panicum, quackgrass, common milkweed, johnsongrass, and common lambsquarters. At present, the most troublesome weeds in the croplands of Kentucky are johnsongrass, giant foxtail, common cocklebur, fall panicum, giant ragweed, large crabgrass, musk thistle, common ragweed, and wild garlic.

During my tenure as curator of the University of Kentucky College of Agriculture Herbarium I did field research and was called upon to identify plants sent to the College by farmers, county extension agents, chemical company representatives, and homeowners. It is from these sources, as well as from botanists and from weed books of the United States, that I have gathered the material for this guide.

About This Book

This guide is intended to assist anyone wishing to identify a weed in Kentucky. Weed identification is a necessary first step in implementing an appropriate weed control program. Because optimal strategies to control weeds can change rapidly and vary with location, the manual does not make recommendations on this topic. Questions about weed control are best directed to county extension agents and weed control specialists.

The plants in this guide are grouped by flower color. The reader will find, however, that many flowers in a given color category have strong tinges of another color. If a plant is not found in one section, the reader is urged to look for it in a closely related color category. A secondary division within each color category is based on the disposition of the leaves on the stem. The reader should determine first the flower color, then whether the plant has alternate, opposite, basal, or whorled leaves. I hope this arrangement will simplify weed identification.

The botanical descriptions are written with the non-botanist in mind. Most of the descriptions have one species per page. If more than one species is included in a particular description, only a few distinguishing characteristics are given for each species below the first one described.

The ranges of the 160 weeds described in this guide are given for Kentucky only. Many of these weeds are found in the neighboring states of Illinois, Indiana, Missouri, Ohio, Tennessee, Virginia, and West Virginia. A weed found in a border region of Kentucky can be expected to occur in the adjacent state also.

Gray's Manual of Botany, 8th edition, by M.L. Fernald, is the source of most of the scientific names. If another name is used in the description, the name from *Gray's Manual* is given as a synonym in brackets. I have used the *Composite List of Weeds*, published by the *Journal of Weed Science Society of America*, as the source of common names.

Abbreviations

mm : millimeter(s) (= 0.039 inch)

cm : centimeter(s) (= 0.39 inch)

dm : decimeter(s) (= 3.9 inches)

m : meter(s) (= 39 inches, 3.3 feet)

syn. : synonym

var : variety

Plant Structures

Parts of a Grass

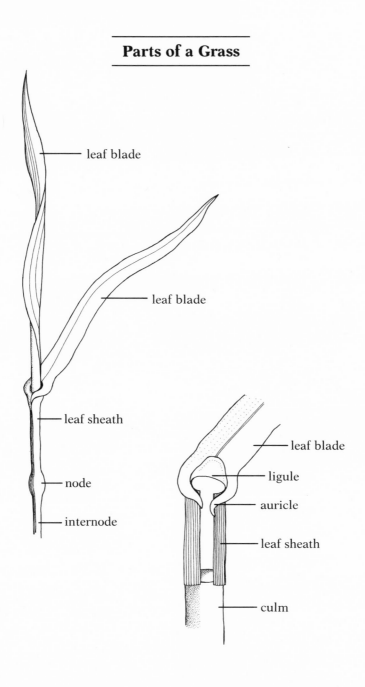

Leaf Arrangement

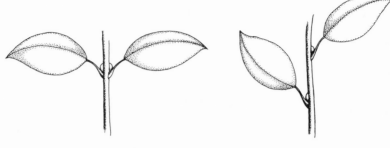

Opposite   Alternate

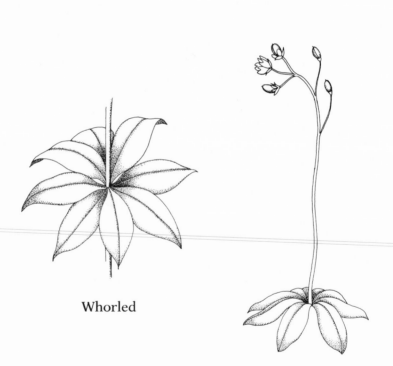

Whorled   Basal

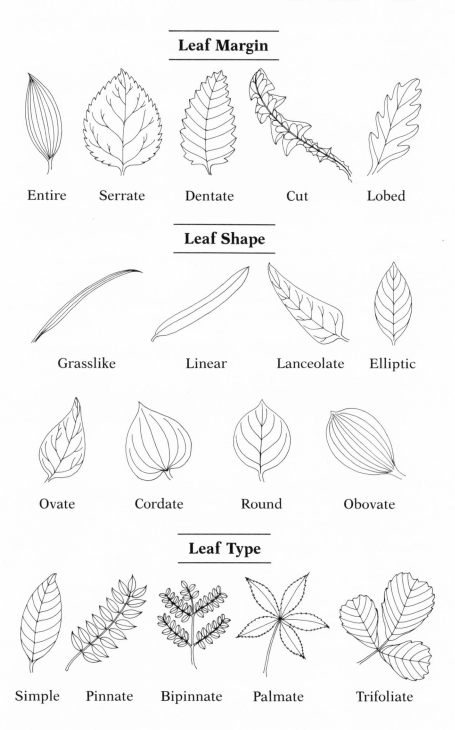

Leaf Margin

Entire   Serrate   Dentate   Cut   Lobed

Leaf Shape

Grasslike   Linear   Lanceolate   Elliptic

Ovate   Cordate   Round   Obovate

Leaf Type

Simple   Pinnate   Bipinnate   Palmate   Trifoliate

Parts of a Complete Flower

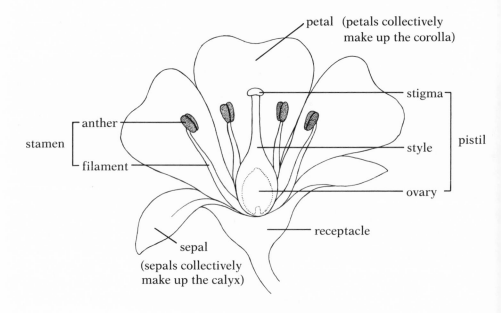

Flowerhead in Asteraceae

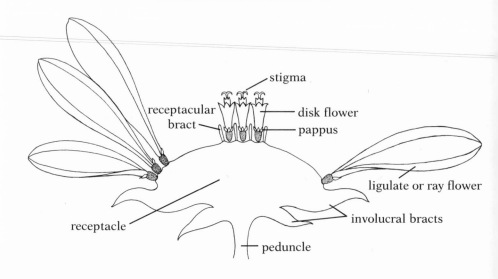

Flower Arrangement

Solitary

Spike

Raceme

Panicle

Umbel

Head and Rays

Flower Form

Round Flat
(radially symmetric)

Cup

Funnel

Two-lipped

Tubular

Plant
Descriptions

White Flowers

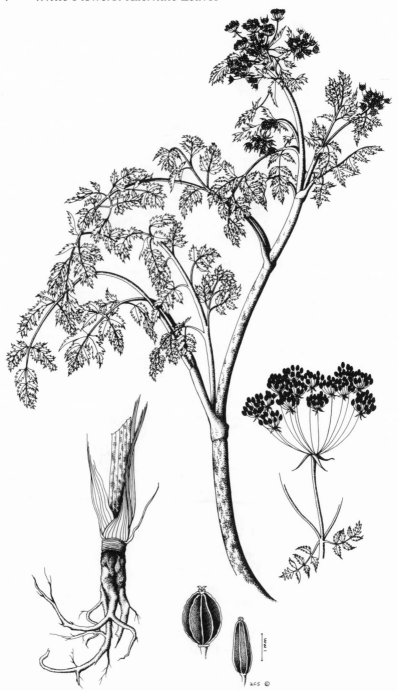

Poison Hemlock
Conium maculatum

Poison Hemlock

Parsley Family

Conium maculatum L.

Apiaceae

EARMARKS.   Plant gives off a rank odor when crushed; leaves finely divided; flowers white, tiny, in numerous umbels.

ORIGIN.   Eurasia.

LIFE CYCLE.   Monocarpic perennial.

STEMS.   Erect, smooth, hollow, purple mottled, and up to 3 m tall.

LEAVES.   Alternate and basal, the lower ones up to 5 dm long (the upper ones progressively smaller), broadly triangular-ovate, and 3-4 times pinnately divided; the enlarged petiole base sheathes the stem.

FLOWERS.   In large, open, compound umbels that are 4-6 cm wide and made up of many flowers. Blooms June through July.

FRUITS.   Pale brown, ovoid, flattened on one side, rounded on the other two, ribbed, and 2-3 mm long.

DISTRIBUTION.   Gardens, waste places, vacant lots, old fields, pastures, woodland borders, roadsides, and railroad embankments throughout the state. Poison hemlock is especially common on limestone soils in northern and central Kentucky.

The generic name is derived from the Greek word *konas*, which means "to whirl about." This weed has been used as a medicine and poison since 500 B.C. It is believed that the Greek philosopher Socrates was put to death by drinking a decoction of this plant. The whole plant is poisonous, and the fruit contains the greatest concentration of alkaloids. The leaves are mistaken often for those of parsley, the roots for those of parsnip, and the seeds for those of anise. Even the hollow stems fashioned into whistles have poisoned children. The plant is poisonous also to livestock.

Wild Carrot

Daucus carota L.

Parsley Family

Apiaceae

EARMARKS. Plant arises from a carrot-like taproot; leaves finely divided; flowers white, tiny, in flat-topped umbels.

ORIGIN. Eurasia.

LIFE CYCLE. Biennial or summer annual.

STEMS. Erect, ridged, hollow, bristly-hairy, and 3-15 dm tall.

LEAVES. In a basal rosette the first year, long-stalked and divided into narrow, lobed segments; stem leaves are alternate and clasping.

FLOWERS. In delicate, compound, flat-topped umbels; there is usually one dark purple flower in the center of each umbel. Blooms June through September.

FRUITS. Yellowish brown, 2-4 mm long, oval, ridged, and prickly on the margin.

DISTRIBUTION. Roadsides, railroad embankments, meadows, thickets, pastures, clearcuts, waste places, gardens, and fallow and cultivated fields throughout the state.

Wild carrot is known also as *queen anne's lace* because the finely-cut, lacy leaves were often used in fashionable head-dresses and bouquets of the seventeenth, eighteenth, and nineteenth centuries. Dried decorations are still made with the umbels and leaves. Two other descriptive names for this plant are *bird's nest* and *bee's nest* because when the seeds ripen, the umbels contract gracefully into the shape of a hollow cup or nest. The seeds of wild carrot have been used in folk medicine in the belief that they bring about conception.

Wild Carrot
Daucus carota

Common Yarrow
Achillea millefolium L.

Composite Family
Asteraceae

EARMARKS. Leaves aromatic when crushed; flower heads white, or occasionally pink, with yellow centers, in dense, flat-topped clusters.

ORIGIN. Europe.

LIFE CYCLE. Perennial herb.

STEMS. Simple to slightly branched, hairy, and 3-10 dm tall.

LEAVES. Alternate, stalkless, 2-14 cm long, and finely divided into short, tiny, feathery, greyish green segments.

FLOWER HEADS. Three to 5 mm wide; at the base of each flower head are several straw-colored, hairy bracts. Blooms June through September.

FRUITS. Small, oblong, whitish grey, seedlike achenes 2-3 mm long.

DISTRIBUTION. Pastures, waste places, fields, thickets, and roadsides throughout the state.

Fossil records of the common yarrow have been found in Neanderthal burial caves, suggesting that it has been associated with humans for at least 60,000 years.

The genus *Achillea* is said to be named for Achilles, who used this herb to treat wounded soldiers during the siege of Troy. This plant has been recognized throughout history for its alleged ability to heal wounds. In the sixteenth century it was called *nosebleed* because the crushed leaves packed into the nostrils were said to stop nosebleeds. In the 1950s, an alkaloid from the plant was found to enhance the clotting of blood.

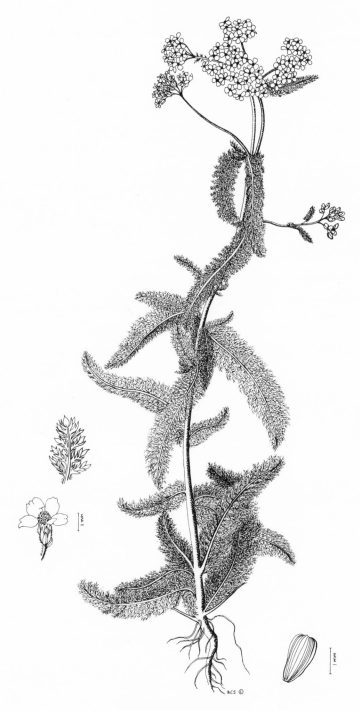

Common Yarrow
Achillea millefolium

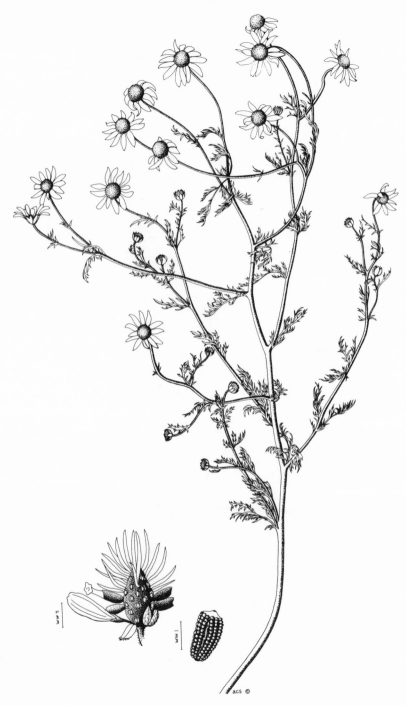

Mayweed Chamomile
Anthemis cotula

Mayweed Chamomile
Anthemis cotula L.

Composite Family
Asteraceae

EARMARKS. Plant strong-scented; leaves alternate, divided into threadlike segments; flower heads white with yellow centers, daisylike.

ORIGIN. Europe.

LIFE CYCLE. Winter annual.

STEMS. Erect, bushy-branched, hairy, and 2-6 cm tall.

LEAVES. Stalkless, yellowish green, hairy, and finely pinnately divided.

FLOWER HEADS. Solitary, terminal, and 12-30 mm wide; the base of the flower head is enclosed by many greenish, hairy bracts. Blooms May through July.

FRUITS. Light brown, bumpy, corncoblike, beaked, seedlike achenes less than 2 mm long.

DISTRIBUTION. Barnyards, pastures, and cultivated fields throughout the state. Mayweed chamomile is especially troublesome in pastures.

This odoriferous barnyard weed often causes severe cases of dermatitis to susceptible persons who come into contact with the leaves, stems, and flowers. Shunned by sheep, hogs, and cattle, mayweed chamomile is said to repel even fleas, bees, and mosquitoes.

The name *cotula* is derived from the Greek *kotyle*, which means "hollow" or "little cup" and refers to the shape of the opening flower heads.

White Heath Aster
Aster pilosus Willd.

Composite Family
Asteraceae

EARMARKS.   Leaves narrow and progressively smaller up the stem; flower heads white to pink with yellow centers.

ORIGIN.   United States.

LIFE CYCLE.   Perennial herb.

STEMS.   Stiffly branched at the base, smooth to white-hairy, and 1-1.5 dm tall.

FLOWER HEADS.   Numerous; each is made up of 20-40 tubular flowers surrounded by white to pink petallike ray flowers, subtended by many narrow, overlapping bracts. Blooms late August through October.

FRUITS.   Light brown, slightly nerved, seedlike achenes 0.7-1.3 mm long.

DISTRIBUTION.   Old fields, woodland thickets, waste places, pastures, gardens, and roadsides throughout the state.

According to myth, asters were created out of stardust, hence the old English name *star-wort*. These plants are known also as *goodbye meadow* because they can crowd out other vegetation.

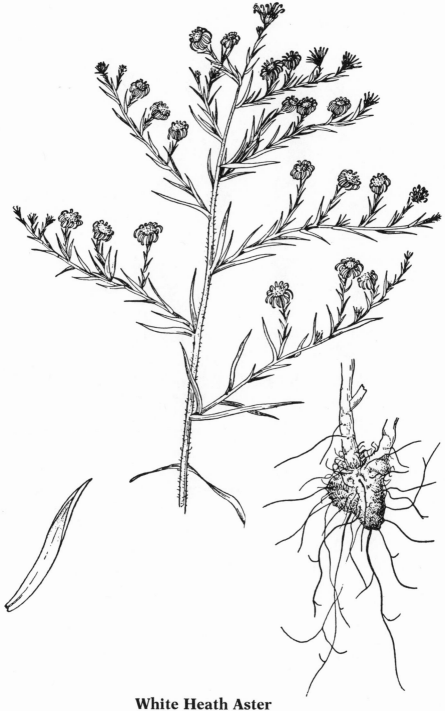

White Heath Aster
Aster pilosus

Qxeye Daisy
Chrysanthemum leucanthemum var. *pinnatifidum*

Oxeye Daisy

Composite Family

Chrysanthemum leucanthemum L.
var. *pinnatifidum* Lecoq & Lamotte

Asteraceae

EARMARKS. Leaves alternate, deeply cut, lobed; flower heads white, solitary, long stalked, daisylike.

ORIGIN. Europe.

LIFE CYCLE. Perennial herb.

STEMS. Erect, smooth, simple to forked near the top, and up to 8 dm tall.

LEAVES. Variable; the basal leaves are deeply cut or lobed and unevenly toothed; the middle and upper leaves are alternate, narrowly oblong, and entire to slightly toothed.

FLOWER HEADS. Terminal, about 3.5 cm wide, and white with a yellow center; the base of each flower head is enclosed by many greenish bracts. Blooms May through late August.

FRUITS. Narrow, dark brown to black with light grey longitudinally ribbed, seedlike achenes 1-1.5 mm long and knobbed at the apex.

DISTRIBUTION. Roadsides, fields, pastures, waste places, clearcuts, and meadows throughout the state.

It is believed that the first oxeye daisy seeds were brought to this country in sacks of grain shipped from England to feed General Burgoyne's horses before the battle at Saratoga.

This common summer plant grows on exhausted pastureland. Livestock such as horses, sheep, and goats often browse on it, but cattle are usually repelled by its pungent, bitter taste. The milk of cows that have eaten the plant is said to have an unpleasant taste.

Oxeye daisy is known also as *moon daisy* because of the appearance of the opening flower heads.

Horseweed

Composite Family

Conyza canadensis (L.) Cronq.   Asteraceae
[Syn. *Erigeron canadensis* L.]

EARMARKS. Leaves alternate, toothed; flower heads small, whitish or greenish with a yellowish center, arranged in a loosely spreading inflorescence.

ORIGIN. United States.

LIFE CYCLE. Winter annual.

STEMS. Erect, usually simple, hairy, and 2-20 dm tall.

LEAVES. Variable; the lower ones are stalked and spatulate, and wither before maturity; the upper ones are smaller, narrow, mostly entire, hairy, clasping, and crowded on the stem.

FLOWER HEADS. Numerous, with as many as 100 minute flowers making up one head; below each flower head are numerous, slender, green bracts. Blooms July through October.

FRUITS. Straw-colored, seedlike achenes 1 mm long, broadest at the whitish-hairy tip.

DISTRIBUTION. Roadsides, waste places, pastures, gardens, and fallow and cultivated fields throughout the state.

Horseweed has a strong, pungent odor caused by a volatile terpene oil secreted by thousands of dotlike glands. The oil may cause inflammation and irritation to the skin and to mucous membranes of the mouth, nose, and eyes in some persons. The plant is said to irritate the nostrils and throats of grazing animals.

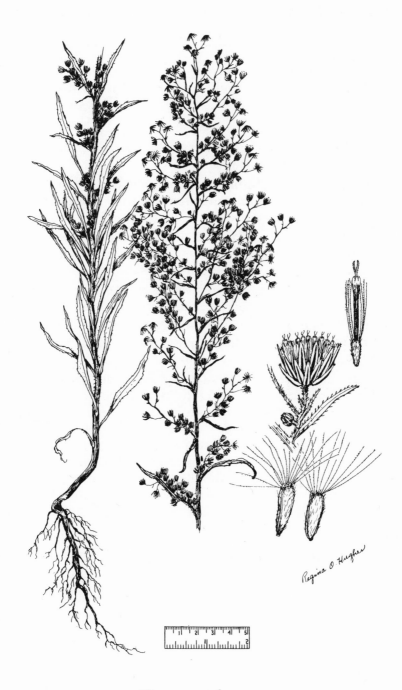

Horseweed
Conyza canadensis

Annual Fleabane
Erigeron annuus (L.) Pers.

Composite Family
Asteraceae

EARMARKS.   Leaves alternate, toothed or entire; flower heads white or purplish pink with yellow centers, daisylike.

ORIGIN.   United States.

LIFE CYCLE.   Winter annual.

STEMS.   Erect, leafy, hairy, branched at the tip, and up to 15 dm tall.

LEAVES.   Small, clasping, lanceolate to elliptic, and pointed at the tip; lower ones are broad, sharply toothed, tapering into a margined stalk, and up to 10 cm long.

FLOWER HEADS.   Numerous, stalked, and 1.5-2 cm wide; the base of each flower head is enclosed by several greenish, slender bracts. Blooms July through September.

FRUITS.   Straw-colored, obovate, seedlike achenes that are somewhat flattened, with an outer crown of short scales and an inner crown of bristly white hairs at the tip.

DISTRIBUTION.   Roadsides, pastures, waste places, gardens, and fallow and cultivated fields throughout the state.

SIMILAR SPECIES.   Philadelphia fleabane, *Erigeron philadelphicus* L., a perennial herb, has clasping stem leaves that are toothed, oblong to ovate, and reduced upwards. The broad flower heads, which nod in bud, are more showy than the other two species and are deep pink to white. Blooms in April through July. Rough fleabane, *Erigeron strigosus* Muhl., a summer annual, has fewer stem leaves. Grows only to 7 dm tall. Blooms in June through August. Both species are common throughout Kentucky.

The generic name is derived from the Greek words *eri* (early) and *geron* (old man) and refers to the grey appearance of some of the species.

Annual Fleabane
Erigeron annuus

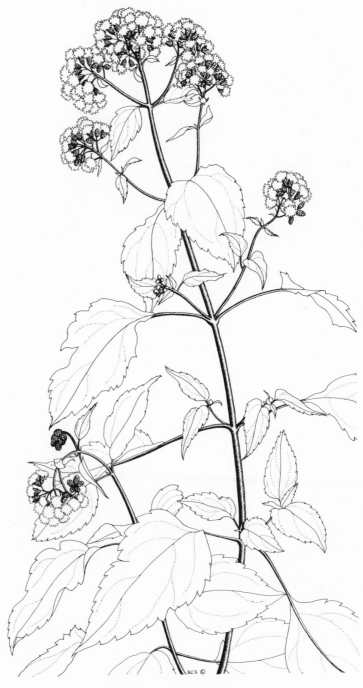

White Snakeroot
Eupatorium rugosum

White Snakeroot
Eupatorium rugosum Houtt.

Composite Family
Asteraceae

EARMARKS. Leaves opposite, stalked; flower heads white, in broad loosely arranged clusters.

ORIGIN. United States.

LIFE CYCLE. Perennial herb.

STEMS. Erect, simple to much-branched, smooth to slightly hairy, and up to 1.5 m tall.

LEAVES. Ovate, 6-18 cm long, sharply toothed, and tapered to a long tip.

FLOWER HEADS. Emerging from the leaf axils and at the tips of the branches; they contain 12-24 small flowers 3-4 mm long; the base of each flower head is enclosed by several greenish bracts. Blooms August through September.

FRUITS. Black or dark brown, linear, seedlike achenes 2-2.5 mm long.

DISTRIBUTION. Woodland borders, moist meadows, thickets, pastures, fencerows, riverbanks, and roadsides throughout the state.

SIMILAR SPECIES. Late boneset, *Eupatorium serotinum* Michx., a perennial herb, has broadly lanceolate to ovate leaves that are 3–5 nerved, toothed, and long-stalked. The whitish to pale purple flowers are in fuzzy clusters that bloom from August through September.

Eupatorium was named by Linnaeus in honor of the Greek physician Eupator Mithridates, who made medicine from one of the species in the genus.

White snakeroot has long been a problem to livestock that eat it when other forage is scarce. Cattle that graze on it may develop "trembles," or "milk sickness." The plant contains a poison called *tremetol*, which is soluble in milk fat and may be transferred to suckling animals or to humans drinking the milk from the affected animal. The symptoms include nausea, vomiting, weakness, slow respiration, and possibly collapse. This disease is believed to have been responsible for the death of Abraham Lincoln's mother.

Corn Gromwell
Lithospermum arvense L.

Borage Family
Boraginaceae

EARMARKS. Plant downy; leaves alternate, entire; flowers white to pale pink, in short to long clusters.

ORIGIN. Europe.

LIFE CYCLE. Winter annual.

STEMS. Erect, simple or branched at the base, leafy above, and up to 7 dm tall.

LEAVES. Entire, narrow, stalkless, and up to 3 cm long.

FLOWERS. Tubular, 5-7 mm long, and nearly stalkless in the axils of the upper, leafy bracts. Blooms April through May.

FRUITS. Four or fewer small, conical, greyish tan nutlets 3 mm long with many white bumps and a dark brown scar at the base.

DISTRIBUTION. Gardens, old fields, waste places, and fallow and cultivated fields throughout the state. Corn gromwell is especially common in grain fields.

The generic name is derived from the Greek word for "stone seed" and refers to the stonelike appearance of the seeds.

Corn Gromwell
Lithospermum arvense

Field Pepperweed
Lepidium campestre (L.) R. Br.

Mustard Family
Brassicaceae

EARMARKS.   Leaves alternate on the stem, with clasping arrow-shaped leaf bases; flowers white, tiny; seed pods broad, roundish.

ORIGIN.   Europe.

LIFE CYCLE.   Winter annual.

STEMS.   Erect, branched above, greyish hairy, very leafy, and 2-6 dm tall.

LEAVES.   Variable; the lower ones, in a rosette, are entire or lobed; the upper ones are stalkless and entire to toothed.

FLOWERS.   Inconspicuous; they are crowded in dense clusters at the tip of the branches and have 4 sepals, 4 petals, and 6 stamens. Blooms April and May and sporadically until early fall.

FRUITS.   Roundish, oblong-ovate pods 5-6 mm long; each half has one dark brown, obovoid seed 2-2.5 mm long.

DISTRIBUTION.   Roadsides, gardens, waste places, thickets, pastures, and fallow and cultivated fields throughout the state.

SIMILAR SPECIES.   Virginia pepperweed, *Lepidium virginicum* L., a winter annual, has basal leaves and alternate, linear stem leaves that are arrow-shaped at the base. The circular seed pods are 2.5-4 mm long with a style projecting from the notched summit. Blooms in April and May and sporadically until early fall.

The seeds of both species are relished by small birds, hence the common names *birdseed* and *bird's pepper*. The leaves and immature seed pods of virginia pepperweed may be gathered in the spring and used as seasoning or cooked as greens.

Field Pepperweed
Lepidium campestre

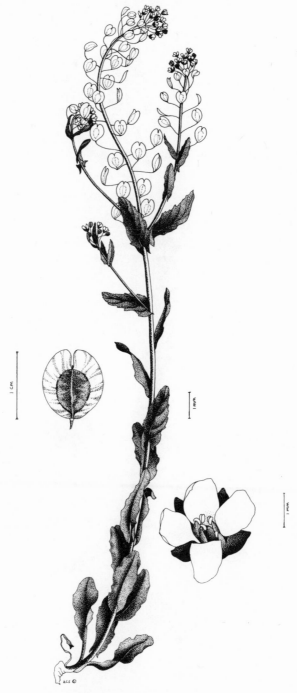

Field Pennycress
Thlaspi arvense

Field Pennycress
Thlaspi arvense L.

Mustard Family
Brassicaceae

EARMARKS. Leaves alternate with arrow-shaped leaf bases clasping the stem; flowers white, tiny; seed pods circular, flat.

ORIGIN. Eurasia.

LIFE CYCLE. Winter annual.

STEMS. Smooth, simple to branched above, and up to 8 dm tall.

LEAVES. Simple, slightly toothed, and 1.3-5 cm long; the lower leaves are stalked and the upper ones have arrow-shaped leaf bases.

FLOWERS. In clusters that elongate at maturity; each flower has 4 sepals and 4 petals arranged in the form of a cross. Blooms April through June.

FRUITS. Seed pods 1 cm wide, broadly winged, and notched at the top; they contain many brown or black seeds 2-3 mm long.

DISTRIBUTION. Roadsides, waste places, pastures, gardens, and fallow and cultivated fields throughout the state.

The young leaves of the field pennycress, when cut into small pieces, can be a tasty addition to green salads, and the dried, crushed seeds can add zest to any meal. The dried seed pods are used for winter bouquets.

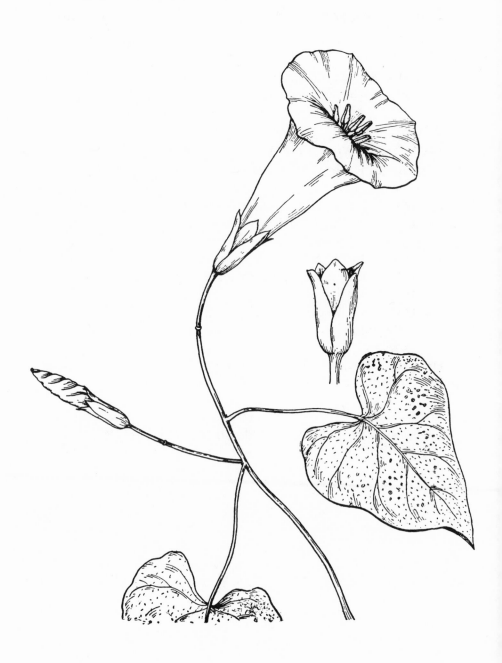

Bigroot Morningglory
Ipomoea pandurata

Bigroot Morningglory

Ipomoea pandurata (L.)
G.F.W. Mey.

Morningglory Family
Convolvulaceae

EARMARKS. Plant is a vine; leaves alternate, heart-shaped; flowers white with purple centers; sepals smooth.

ORIGIN. United States.

LIFE CYCLE. Perennial vine.

STEMS. Trailing or twining, purplish, smooth to slightly hairy, and up to 3 m long.

LEAVES. Entire, long-stalked, 2-lobed at the base, sharp-pointed, and 5-15 cm long.

FLOWERS. Showy and in clusters of 1-7 on long stalks, each with 5 blunt-tipped sepals and 5 petals that form a tube 5-8 cm long. Blooms June through September.

FRUITS. Capsules enclosed by leaflike sepals; they contain blackish brown seeds 6-7 mm long with 1 rounded surface and 2 flat surfaces.

DISTRIBUTION. Roadsides, riverbanks, thickets, fencerows, and fallow and cultivated fields throughout the state.

This species is also aptly named *man-under-ground* and *man-of-the-earth*, references to the hugh edible storage roots that can weigh up to 29 lbs. Although these roots are deeply hidden underground, digging them out is worth the effort because they are valuable sources of starch.

Pitted Morningglory

Ipomoea lacunosa L.

Morningglory Family

Convolvulaceae

EARMARKS.   Plant is a vine; leaves alternate, heart-shaped at the base; flowers white, small; sepals hairy.

ORIGIN.   Tropical North America.

LIFE CYCLE.   Summer annual.

STEMS.   Slender, twining, and up to 2 m long.

LEAVES.   Entire, thin, and up to 8 cm long, with a maroon band around the margin.

FLOWERS.   In clusters of two to several on short maroonish stalks; they have 5 hairy, sharp-pointed sepals; the tubular corolla is 1-2 cm long. Blooms July through September.

FRUITS.   Brown capsules; the 4-6 brownish black seeds are about 5 mm long and have 1 rounded surface and 2 flat surfaces.

DISTRIBUTION.   Roadsides, gardens, waste places, turf, thickets, fences, pastures, and fallow and cultivated fields throughout the state.

The generic name is from the Greek *ips*, which means "worm" and refers to the twining habit of the morningglory.

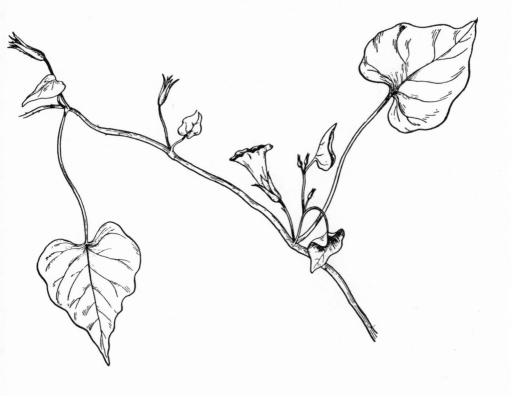

Pitted Morningglory
Ipomoea lacunosa

Field Bindweed
Convolvulus arvensis

Field Bindweed
Convolvulus arvensis L.

Morningglory Family
Convolvulaceae

EARMARKS. Plant is a vine; leaves arrow-shaped at the base; flowers white or pinkish, funnel form; flower stalk has two minute bracts.

ORIGIN. Eurasia.

LIFE CYCLE. Perennial herbaceous vine.

STEMS. Smooth to hairy, slender, prostrate to twining, and up to 3 m tall.

LEAVES. Alternate, simple, 1-5 cm long, and long-stalked, with triangular to arrow-shaped basal lobes.

FLOWERS. On long stalks in the leaf axils; each has 5 small, rounded sepals, 5 united petals, 5 stamens, and 1 pistil with 2 stigmas. Blooms June through September.

FRUITS. Greyish green capsules, 3-angled with 1 side rounded and 2 sides flat; each contains 2-4 seeds.

DISTRIBUTION. Roadsides, waste places, fencerows, pastures, turf, and fallow and cultivated fields throughout the state.

The flowers of field bindweed, which is also called *creeping jenny*, are sensitive to adverse weather conditions and close with approaching rainfall and at night time.

Convolvulus is derived from the Latin *convolare*, which means "to interwine," and is descriptive of its growth habit. The Latin word *arvensis* means "cornfield."

Ivyleaf Morningglory
Ipomoea hederacea (L.) Jacq.

Morningglory Family
Convolvulaceae

EARMARKS. Plant is a vine; leaves alternate, deeply 3-lobed; flowers white, purple, or blue, and funnelform; sepals densely hairy.

ORIGIN. Tropical America.

LIFE CYCLE. Summer annual.

STEMS. Hairy, twining or trailing, and up to 2 m long.

LEAVES. Deeply 3-lobed, sharp-pointed at the tips, rounded or heart-shaped at the bases, and 5-12 cm long.

FLOWERS. One to 3 showy flowers per plant, in the leaf axils; each has 5 slender sepals with recurved tips; the corolla is funnelform and 2.5-5.5 cm long. Blooms late June through September.

FRUITS. Capsules with 4-6 greyish black, densely hairy seeds, 5-5.6 mm long, each with 1 rounded surface, 2 flat surfaces, and a prominent scar at the base.

DISTRIBUTION. Roadsides, waste places, turf, pastures, gardens, fencerows, and fallow and cultivated fields throughout the state.

SIMILAR SPECIES. Entireleaf morningglory, *Ipomoea hederacea* (L.) Jacq. var. *integriuscula* Gray, a summer annual, has leaves that are entire, unlobed, and heart-shaped. Entireleaf morningglory is found throughout Kentucky.

The first mention of morningglories in American garden literature was in 1806 when Bernard McMahon, a Philadelphia nurseryman, advertized nasturtiums and morningglories in his "American Gardener's Calender." This catalog listed new and rare seeds and plants that he had collected from all over the world.

Today, this showy morningglory is often grown as an ornamental vine.

Ivyleaf Morningglory
Ipomoea hederacea

Hedge Bindweed
Calystegia sepium

Hedge Bindweed

Morningglory Family

Calystegia sepium (L.) R. Br.   Convolvulaceae
[Syn. *Convolvulus sepium* L.]

EARMARKS. Plant is a vine; leaves alternate, arrow-shaped at the base; flowers white to rose-colored; 2 large bracts enclose the base of the flower.

ORIGIN. Europe.

LIFE CYCLE. Perennial herb.

STEMS. Twining or trailing, smooth to hairy, and 9-30 dm long.

LEAVES. Simple, long-stalked, and heart-shaped to triangular-ovate; each has two broad basal lobes.

FLOWERS. Showy, funnelform, and 3-6 cm long; they grow on long angular stalks. Blooms June through September.

FRUITS. Three-angled capsules 4-5 mm long, each with 1 side rounded, the other 2 sides flat, containing 2-4 greyish black seeds.

DISTRIBUTION. Roadsides, gardens, fencerows, waste places, thickets, bottomlands, and fallow and cultivated fields throughout the state.

In the *Historia Naturalis* Pliny the Elder, the great herbalist, likened the hedge bindweed to the lily: "for whiteness they resemble one another very much, as if Nature in making this flower were a learning and trying her skill how to frame the Lilly indeed."

The delicate flower resembles a cap and is often called *lady's nightcap*.

White Sweetclover
Melilotus alba Desr.

Legume Family
Fabaceae

EARMARKS. Leaves alternate, with 3 leaflets, the middle leaflet stalked; flowers white, in elongated clusters.

ORIGIN. Eurasia.

LIFE CYCLE. Biennial.

STEMS. Slender, branched, smooth, and up to 2 m tall.

LEAVES. Pale green; each leaflet is oblong, toothed, and usually indented at the tip; the terminal leaflet is stalked.

FLOWERS. Small and pealike. Blooms June through September.

FRUITS. Veiny pods 2-3.5 mm long; they contain one yellowish green to brown, oval seed 2 mm long.

DISTRIBUTION. Pastures, fields, and waste places throughout the state. White sweetclover is often planted along roadsides to help stop soil erosion.

SIMILAR SPECIES. Yellow sweetclover, *Melilotus officinalis* (L.) Lam., a biennial, has yellow flowers and grows in similar habitats.

Furs and clothing packed with either white or yellow sweetclover reputedly provide protection from moths. In addition, a sweet odor is imparted to the garments. Today, the sweetclovers are commonly used in sachets and potpourri mixtures.

White sweetclover was cultivated in the United States as early as 1739. It was first grown as a honey plant but now is also valued for forage, hay, and coverage on bare soil.

Sweetclover poisoning in livestock is caused by the ingestion of moldy sweetclover hay. The plant's toxic substance, *dicoumarin*, causes the animal to die of internal haemorrhage.

White Sweetclover
Melilotus alba

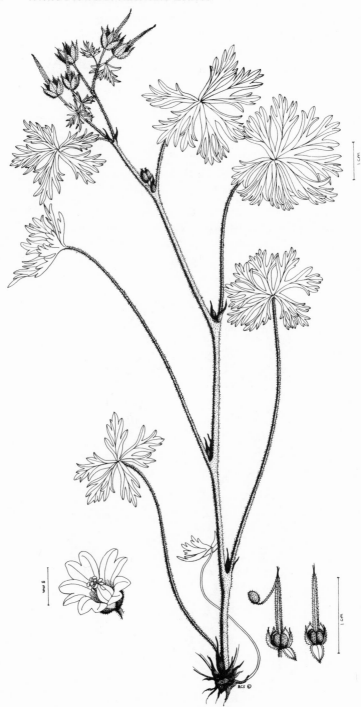

Carolina Geranium
Geranium carolinianum

Carolina Geranium

Geranium carolinianum L.

Geranium Family

Geraniaceae

EARMARKS.　Leaves deeply cleft or lobed; flowers white or pink, in clusters; fruits long, like a cranes bill.

ORIGIN.　United States.

LIFE CYCLE.　Winter annual.

STEMS.　Erect, freely branched, pinkish at the base, hairy, and up to 6 dm tall.

LEAVES.　Alternate or occasionally opposite, deeply palmately cleft, each divided into 5-9 linear-oblong segments.

FLOWERS.　In clusters at the tips of the stem, each with 5 green sepals, 5 petals, 10 stamens, and 1 pistil with a long style. Blooms April through July.

FRUITS.　Capsules with 5 segments that separate elastically from the style; in each segment there is one light brown, oblong, pitted seed 1.6-2.0 mm long.

DISTRIBUTION.　Roadsides, waste places, gardens, old fields, turf, and fallow and cultivated fields throughout the state.

The generic name comes from the Greek word *geranos*, which means "crane" and refers to the resemblance of the slender fruit to the long-billed bird.

The cultivated geranium belongs to the genus *Pelargonium* and is in the same family as this weedy species.

Venice Mallow
Hibiscus trionum

Venice Mallow

Hibiscus trionum L.

Mallow Family

Malvaceae

EARMARKS. Leaves alternate, divided; flowers cream-colored and purple-centered; fruit capsule inflated, dark-veined.

ORIGIN. Europe.

LIFE CYCLE. Summer annual.

STEMS. Erect or spreading, hairy, and 2-5 dm high.

LEAVES. Long-stalked, deeply 3-parted, bluntly or coarsely lobed, and pinnately veined.

FLOWERS. Solitary or in clusters of 2 or 3 in the upper leaf axils; each has 5 sepals and 5 petals; numerous stamens form a cylinder around the pistil. Blooms July through September.

FRUITS. Capsules 1-1.7 cm long, each enclosed by the inflated, bladdery calyx; seeds are dark brown, kidney-shaped, and 2 mm long, with clumps of brownish hairs on the surface.

DISTRIBUTION. Waste places, gardens and fallow and cultivated fields throughout the state.

This beautiful plant is used in old-fashioned flower gardens. It is also called *good-night-at-noon* because the flowers open in the morning and close around noon. If the sky is cloudy they do not open at all.

Common Pokeweed
Phytolacca americana

Common Pokeweed

Pokeweed Family

Phytolacca americana L.

Phytolaccaceae

EARMARKS. Plant tall, succulent; leaves alternate, entire; flowers whitish green, in long clusters.

ORIGIN. United States.

LIFE CYCLE. Perennial herb.

STEMS. Stout, branched, reddish purple, smooth, and 1-3 m tall.

LEAVES. Stalked, simple, broadly oblong-lanceolate to oval, and 1-3 dm long.

FLOWERS. In long nodding clusters at the tips of the branches; each has 5 petallike sepals 5-7 mm wide, usually 10 stamens, and 1 pistil. Blooms July through September.

FRUITS. Ten-seeded, dark purple berries 7-10 mm wide, with glossy black, circular seeds.

DISTRIBUTION. Roadsides, railroad embankments, pastures, fencerows, woodland borders, waste places, clearcuts, and fallow and cultivated fields throughout the state.

Common pokeweed is both a medicinal and a poisonous plant. The roots and seeds are extremely poisonous. It is said that the leaves are probably just as deadly, but when repeatedly boiled in water, the toxin is steeped out and poured off. The tincture of common pokeweed extract was once sold in drugstores as one the best remedies known for reducing caking and swelling of cow udders.

One of the first natural inks used by settlers in the New World was obtained from the fruits of this plant.

Prostrate Knotweed

Polygonum aviculare L.

Knotweed Family

Polygonaceae

EARMARKS. Plant sprawling, with jointed stems; leaves alternate, entire; flowers whitish pink, tiny.

ORIGIN. United States and Eurasia.

LIFE CYCLE. Summer annual.

STEMS. Much-branched, mat-forming, slender, blue-green, longitudinally ridged, and swollen at the joints; they grow to 1 m long.

LEAVES. Bluish green, lanceolate, linear to oblong, and 5-30 mm long; the leaf stalks are short and grow from a distinct papery sheath wrapped around each joint.

FLOWERS. Produced singly or in clusters in the leaf axils; each has 5-6 green sepals, about 8 stamens, and 1 pistil with 3 styles. Blooms June through November.

FRUITS. Reddish brown, oval, 3-angled, 1-seeded, seedlike achenes 2-2.6 mm long.

DISTRIBUTION. Roadsides, gardens, turf, pathways, waste places, and fallow and cultivated fields throughout the state. Prostrate knotweed thrives in compacted soil.

The tiny seeds of this plant may be ground into a flour that is similar to buckwheat and can be used in baking cookies, pancakes, and breads.

In folk medicine, the fresh or dried stems are gathered during the flowering season and used in the belief that they cure diarrhea in farm animals.

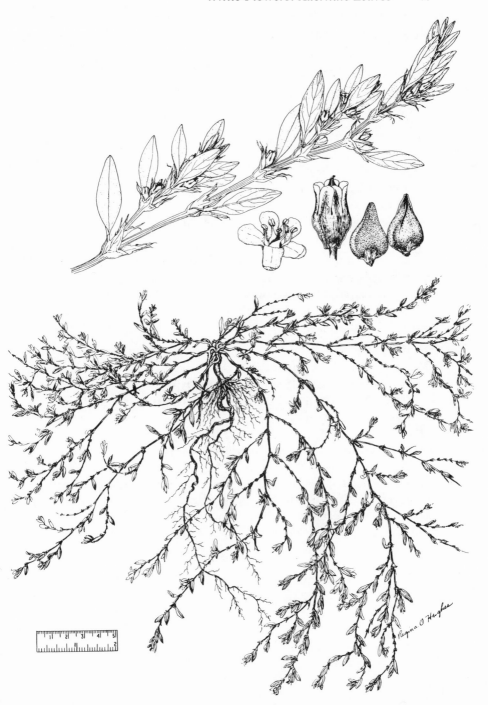

Prostrate Knotweed
Polygonum aviculare

Passionflower
Passiflora incarnata L.

Passionflower Family
Passifloraceae

EARMARKS.   Plant is a tendril-bearing vine; leaves alternate, deeply 3-lobed; flowers showy, whitish green with purple fringe.

ORIGIN.   United States.

LIFE CYCLE.   Perennial herbaceous vine.

STEMS.   Climbing or trailing by axillary tendrils and up to 10 m long.

LEAVES.   Long-stalked, toothed, sharp-pointed, palmately veined, and 6-10 cm long.

FLOWERS.   Axillary, each with 5 reflexed sepals, 5 petals, and a purple and white fringe or crown; the 5 stamens appear to be suspended and surround 1 pistil that has 3-4 drooping stigmas. Blooms June through August.

FRUITS.   Yellow-green, many-seeded, rounded berries 3-5 cm long.

DISTRIBUTION.   Pastures, thickets, fencerows, cultivated fields, woodland borders, riverbottoms, and roadsides throughout the state. Passionflower thrives in sandy soils in open, sunny areas.

In the seventeenth century Jesuit priests from Spain and Italy saw symbols of the crucifixion of Christ in the plant's unique flowers. The five petals and five sepals represented the loyal apostles, the five stamens were Christ's five wounds, the showy corona resembled the crown of thorns that Christ wore, and the leaves represented the hands of Christ's persecutors.

Passionflower
Passiflora incarnata

Balloonvine
Cardiospermum halicacabum

Balloonvine
Soapberry Family
Cardiospermum halicacabum L.   Sapinadaceae

EARMARKS. Plant is a vine; leaves alternate, with three leaflets; flowers white, tiny; fruits are inflated, green capsules.

ORIGIN. Tropical America.

LIFE CYCLE. Summer annual herbaceous vine.

STEMS. Branched and climbing by tendrils; they grow to 3 m long.

LEAVES. Composed of 3 ovate to triangular leaflets with bluntly lobed teeth on the margins and a prominent midvein below.

FLOWERS. About 5 mm wide, asymmetrical, and on long stalks at the tips of the stems or in the leaf axils. Blooms July through September.

FRUITS. Two to 4 cm long, each containing 3 black, smooth seeds each of which has a light-colored, heart-shaped spot.

DISTRIBUTION. Moist open fields, thickets, and cultivated fields throughout the western counties, where it is especially troublesome on bottomlands in the Purchase Area.

Balloonvine is found in the southern United States. It is spreading northward into soybean-producing areas primarily through contaminated soybean seed sold from grower to grower. The seeds are similar in size to those of soybeans and are easily missed in separation procedures.

The young, tender leaves are cooked in some tropical countries as a vegetable.

Jimsonweed
Datura stramonium L.

Nightshade Family
Solanaceae

EARMARKS. Plant strong-scented; flowers large, white or purplish, funnelform; fruits prickly.

ORIGIN. Asia and southern regions of the United States.

LIFE CYCLE. Summer annual.

STEMS. Erect, smooth, green or purplish, branched above, and 3-15 dm tall.

LEAVES. Alternate, long-stalked, 7-20 cm long, dark green above, simple and unevenly toothed or lobed.

FLOWERS. Short-stalked in the leaf axils; each is 6-15 cm long, with 5 green, toothed, angular sepals, 5 united petals, 5 stamens, and a 2-lobed stigma. Blooms June through September.

FRUITS. Hard, prickly capsules that split lengthwise into 4 parts and contain many black, pitted, kidney-shaped seeds about 3 mm long.

DISTRIBUTION. Pastures, barnyards, waste places, and fallow and cultivated fields throughout the state.

The common name is a corruption of "Jamestownweed." According to legend, in 1676 a detachment of British troops was sent to Jamestown to control an uprising. On the journey there, the troops ate some shoots of this weed and were driven mad for several days. Thus, jimsonweed saved the Jamestown colonists from punishment.

The whole plant is poisonous and is known for its mind-altering powers. In folk medicine, it is used as a dangerous ingredient of love potions. It is also called *devil's apple*.

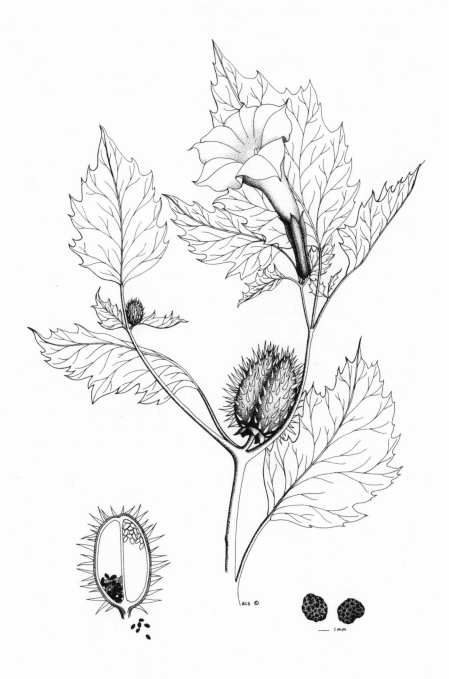

Jimsonweed
Datura stramonium

Eastern Black Nightshade   Nightshade Family
Solanum ptycanthum Dunal ex DC.   Solanaceae

EARMARKS. Leaves alternate; flowers whitish yellow, star-shaped; ripe berries are purplish black.

ORIGIN. United States.

LIFE CYCLE. Summer annual.

STEMS. Freely branching, greenish purple, and up to 1 m tall.

LEAVES. Triangular to elliptic and up to 9 cm long.

FLOWERS. In clusters; there are 5 triangular, unequal sepals, 5 petals, and 5 yellow stamens. Blooms May through September.

FRUITS. Lustrous berries 7-9 mm wide that contain many light, roundish seeds.

DISTRIBUTION. Roadsides, railroad embankments, waste places, pastures, fencerows, gardens, and cultivated fields throughout the state.

Eastern black nightshade is common in North America east of the Rocky Mountains. In Kentucky, it is a troublesome agronomic weed, especially in soybeans. It not only affects production by competing with the crop, but also contaminates the harvested product. The juicy berries often rupture and stain the soybean seeds and cause other debris to stick to them during the harvesting process.

Eastern Black Nightshade
Solanum ptycanthum

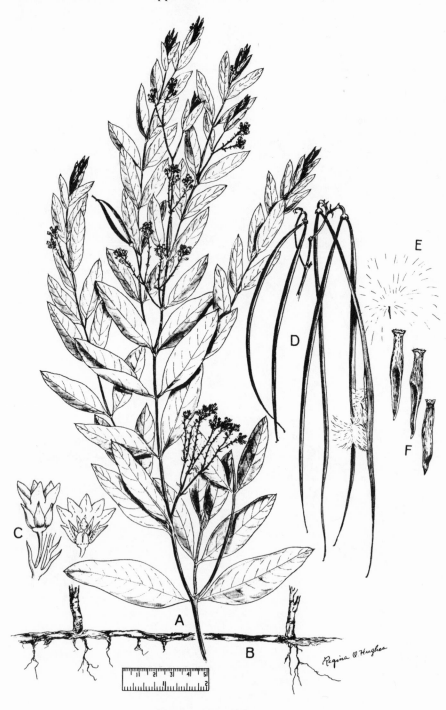

Hemp Dogbane
Apocynum cannabinum

Hemp Dogbane
Apocynum cannabinum L.

Dogbane Family
Apocynaceae

EARMARKS. Plant has milky sap; leaves opposite, dark green above, pale beneath; flowers white or greenish, bell-shaped, in clusters.

ORIGIN. United States.

LIFE CYCLE. Perennial herb.

STEMS. Slightly woody at the base, branched, and up to 6 dm tall.

LEAVES. Simple, oblong-ovate to lanceolate, distinctly veined, and 5-21 cm long.

FLOWERS. In dense terminal clusters 2.5-4 mm long; each has 5 sepals and 5 fused petals. Blooms June through August.

FRUITS. Two pods develop from each flower; these pods are 8-12 cm long, slender, and reddish brown, and contain seeds that have tufts of silky white hairs.

DISTRIBUTION. Roadsides, waste places, dry woodland borders, streambanks, and fallow and cultivated fields throughout the state.

Hemp dogbane is known for the long, brownish fibers from its stems, which are strong, durable, and used in making fish nets, string, and rope. Peter Kalm, a student of Linnaeus's, wrote that Swedish colonists along the Delaware River preferred rope made from *hemp dogbane* to that from common hemp and bought yards of it from the Indians in exchange for a piece of bread.

Fibers from this plant have been identified in Ohio Hopewell and Adena fabrics dating back to 100-300 B.C.

Honeyvine Milkweed

Ampelamus albidus (Nutt.) Britt.
[Syn. *Gonolobus laevis* Michx.]

Milkweed Family

Asclepidaceae

EARMARKS. Plants twining; leaves opposite, heart-shaped; flowers whitish green.

ORIGIN. United States.

LIFE CYCLE. Perennial herb.

STEMS. Smooth and slender, and without milky juice; they grow to 4 m tall.

LEAVES. Long-stalked, dark green, and 3-10 cm wide; each has a wide basal sinus and prominent veins.

FLOWERS. Borne in roundish clusters on long stalks in the leaf axils. Blooms July through September.

FRUITS. Long, smooth, slender green pods 10-15 cm long, which open along one seam and contain many light brown, oval, winged seeds tipped with silky hairs.

DISTRIBUTION. Roadsides, waste places, fencerows, thickets, pastures, and fallow and cultivated fields throughout the state.

Beekeepers recommend this plant as an excellent source of pollen for honey production. However, once established, it can spread easily and become a noxious weed.

Honeyvine Milkweed
Ampelamus albidus

Eclipta

Eclipta prostrata (L.) L.
[Syn. *Eclipta alba* (L.) Hassk.]

Composite Family

Asteraceae

EARMARKS. Leaves opposite, long, narrow; flower heads white with pale yellow centers, daisylike.

ORIGIN. Asia.

LIFE CYCLE. Summer annual.

STEMS. Prostrate to erect, often rooting at the nodes, loosely branched, and 2-9 dm long.

LEAVES. Lanceolate to oblong, 2-10 cm long, slightly toothed, and sharply pointed.

FLOWER HEADS. One or two at the tips of the branches and less than 1 cm wide; the base of each flower head is encircled by several greenish bracts. Blooms July through September.

FRUITS. Golden brown, oblong to squarish, bumpy, 3-4 sided, seedlike achenes with tufts of short white hairs at the summit.

DISTRIBUTION. Damp soils, roadside ditches, pond margins, waste places, and fallow and cultivated fields throughout the state.

Eclipta is derived from the Greek *ekleipsis*, which means "lacking, obscure," and refers to the inconspicuous white ray flowers. Another name is *yerba de tago*. In Spanish, *yerba* means "herb," and *tago* means "ditch." This name makes reference to the frequent occurence of the plants along ditches and other wet sites.

Eclipta is used as an astringent and is said to stop bleeding and promote healing of cuts. The crushed plant, rubbed on the skin, is said to be an excellent cure for skin diseases. It also yields a blackish blue dye, which in India is used for hair coloring and tatooing.

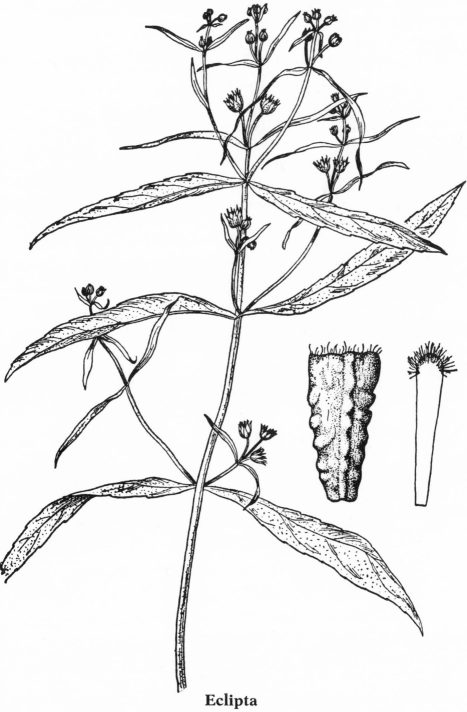

Eclipta
Eclipta prostrata

Hairy Galinsoga

Composite Family

Galinsoga quadriradiata Ruiz & Pavon

Asteraceae

[Syn. *Galinsoga ciliata* (Raf.) Blake]

EARMARKS.   Plant densely covered with white hairs; leaves opposite or whorled, toothed; flower heads tiny, daisylike, white around the edge, yellow-centered.

ORIGIN.   Tropical America.

LIFE CYCLE.   Summer annual.

STEMS.   Erect or spreading, rough, hairy, often glandular, and from 3-6 cm tall.

LEAVES.   Stalked, ovate, 3-nerved, toothed, and 2-8 cm long.

FLOWER HEADS.   Numerous and delicate; the base of each flower head is enclosed by several greenish bracts. Blooms June through September.

FRUITS.   Densely hairy, dark brown, seedlike achenes; widest at the apex and up to 1.5 mm long.

DISTRIBUTION.   Roadsides, gardens, turf, pastures, waste places, and fallow and cultivated fields throughout the state. Hairy galinsoga is especially troublesome in low-growing vegetable crops.

This common weed is named for Mariano Martinez de Galinsoga, a Spanish botanist of the eighteenth century.

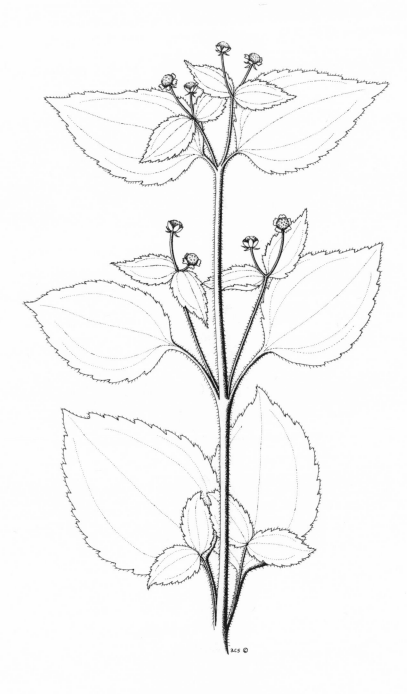

Hairy Galinsoga
Galinsoga quadriradiata

Mouseear Chickweed
Cerastium fontanum

Mouseear Chickweed

Cerastium fontanum Baumg.
[Syn. *Cerastium vulgatum* L.]

Pink Family
Caryophyllaceae

EARMARKS. Plant mat-forming; leaves opposite, entire; flowers white, with 5 notched petals.

ORIGIN. Eurasia.

LIFE CYCLE. Perennial herb.

STEMS. Sticky, hairy, slender, erect or spreading, and often rooting at the lower nodes; they grow to 5 dm long.

LEAVES. In pairs of 3-7; they are oblong to oval, hairy, 1-nerved, and 1-2 cm long.

FLOWERS. Located at the branch tips; each is small, with 5 sepals and 5 petals 4-6 mm long. Blooms April and May and sporadically until November.

FRUITS. Curved cylindrical capsules 8-10 mm long, containing many minute, reddish brown, knobby seeds.

DISTRIBUTION. Turf, gardens, pastures, fields, woods, moist meadows, fallow and cultivated fields, and roadsides throughout the state.

SIMILAR SPECIES. Nodding chickweed, *Cerastium nutans* Raf., is a weak-stemmed winter annual with petals equal to or exceeding the sepals. Blooms late March through May.

The generic name comes from the Greek word *keras*, which means "horn" and refers to the hornlike seed capsules.

Several species of *Cerastium* are used in landscaping for edgings and rock gardens.

Common Chickweed
Stellaria media

Common Chickweed
Stellaria media (L.) Vill.

Pink Family
Caryophyllaceae

EARMARKS. Leaves opposite, entire; flowers white, with deeply notched petals.

ORIGIN. Eurasia.

LIFE CYCLE. Winter annual.

STEMS. Erect or mat-forming, often rooting at the nodes, and with vertical lines of hairs; they grow to 8 dm tall.

LEAVES. Variable; the upper ones are simple, ovate to elliptic, sharp-pointed, clasping, and 1-3 cm long; the lower ones are similar but short-stalked and hairy at the base.

FLOWERS. Delicate and single or in small clusters at the tips of the stems; each has 5 sepals that are longer than the 5 petals, 3-10 stamens, and 1 pistil with 3-4 styles. Blooms in spring, but is capable of flowering all year round.

FRUITS. Ovoid capsules, 5-7 mm long, that contain dull reddish brown seeds, each 1 mm wide and with curved rows of bumps on the surface.

DISTRIBUTION. Roadsides, turf, gardens, damp woods, pastures, vacant lots, thickets, waste places, and fallow and cultivated fields throughout the state.

An old wives' remedy said to be effective against obesity was to drink common chickweed water or tea. It was also used for troubled stomachs.

This weed is rich in copper, phosphorous, and iron and is eaten as a salad green or vegetable in many countries.

It is also relished for food by wild birds as well as domestic fowl.

Nodding Spurge

Spurge Family

Chamaesyce nutans (Lag.) Small
[Syn. *Euphorbia nutans* Lag.]

Euphorbiaceae

EARMARKS. Plant has milky juice; leaves opposite, entire to slightly toothed, often with a purple blotch in the center; flowers white or, rarely, red, and inconspicuous.

ORIGIN. United States.

LIFE CYCLE. Summer annual.

STEMS. Simple to much-branched and up to 1 m tall.

LEAVES. Oblong to elliptic, with smooth blades, except for a few long hairs at the base; the margins are slightly toothed and the leaf bases are unequal.

FLOWERS. Solitary or in clusters, each a cup-like structure with petal-like appendages. Blooms July through September.

FRUITS. Smooth, 3-lobed capsules, 1.9-2.3 mm long with dark brown, 3-sided, wrinkled seeds.

DISTRIBUTION. Roadsides, waste places, railroad embankments, gardens, pastures, turf, and fallow and cultivated fields, especially in small vegetable crops, throughout the state.

SIMILAR SPECIES. Prostrate spurge, *Euphorbia humistrata* Engelm. ex Gray, has hairy stems that are prostrate. The petal-like appendages are white and the fruit capsule is hairy. Common throughout Kentucky.

Many species in the genus *Euphorbia* have toxins that are known to cause poisoning in humans and livestock. These toxins cause severe irritation and lesions in the mouth, stomach, and intestines.

The name spurge comes from the Latin *espurgare*, meaning "to purge or cleanse," referring to the purgative properties of these plants.

Nodding Spurge

Chamaesyce nutans

Poorjoe
Diodia teres Walt.

Madder Family
Rubiaceae

EARMARKS. Plant erect; leaves opposite, narrow; flowers white to pale purple in the leaf axils; stipules long, bristlelike.

ORIGIN. United States.

LIFE CYCLE. Summer annual.

STEMS. Hairy, 4-angled at the top, and 2-8 cm long.

LEAVES. Two to 4 cm long, stiff, and narrow, clasping the stem.

FLOWERS. Single or in clusters; they are funnelform and 5 mm long. Blooms July through August.

FRUITS. Obovoid nutlets that split into two seeds; the light brown seeds are 3-4 mm long, hairy, ribbed, and crowned with 3-4 persistent sepals.

DISTRIBUTION. Roadsides, waste places, turf, gardens, pastures, and fallow and cultivated fields throughout the state.

SIMILAR SPECIES. Virginia buttonweed, *Diodia virginiana* L., a perennial herb, has elliptic to oblong-lanceolate leaves. There are 2 sepals and the fruits are smooth to hairy. This species is more common in wetter sites.

There are several common names for this plant. *Poorjoe* refers to its preferred habitat—poor soil. *Buttonweed* describes the shape of its buttonlike fruits.

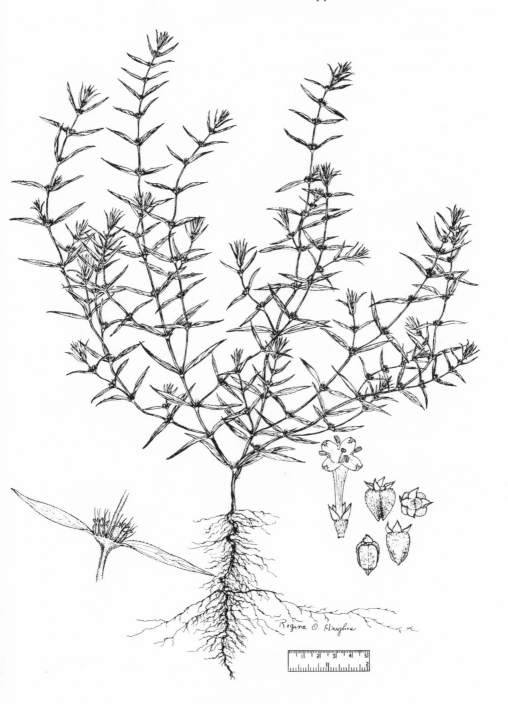

Poorjoe
Diodia teres

White Vervain

Verbena urticifolia L.

Vervain Family

Verbenaceae

EARMARKS.   Leaves opposite, coarsely toothed; flowers white, small, in slender, stiffly ascending clusters.

ORIGIN.   United States.

LIFE CYCLE.   Perennial herb.

STEMS.   Erect, angled, with a few ascending branches, slightly hairy, and 5-15 dm tall.

LEAVES.   Short-stalked, oval to oblong-ovate, unevenly toothed, long-pointed, and 8-20 cm long.

FLOWERS.   Tubular and evenly spaced on the branches of the clusters; there are 5 sepals and 5 petals, each about 2 mm wide. Blooms June through September.

FRUITS.   Oval, reddish brown nutlets 1.5 mm long.

DISTRIBUTION.   Roadsides, railroad embankments, ditches, moist meadows, thickets, waste places, woodland borders, and fencerows throughout the state.

The word *verbena* is derived from the Latin *verber*, which means "rod," "stick," or "stem." In some parts of the country, the stems have been used to sprinkle holy water.

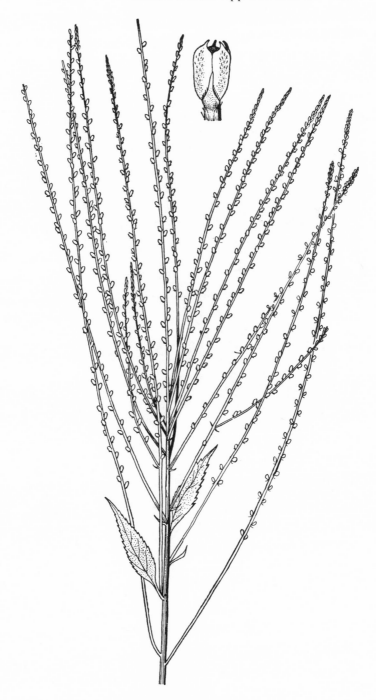

White Vervain
Verbena urticifolia

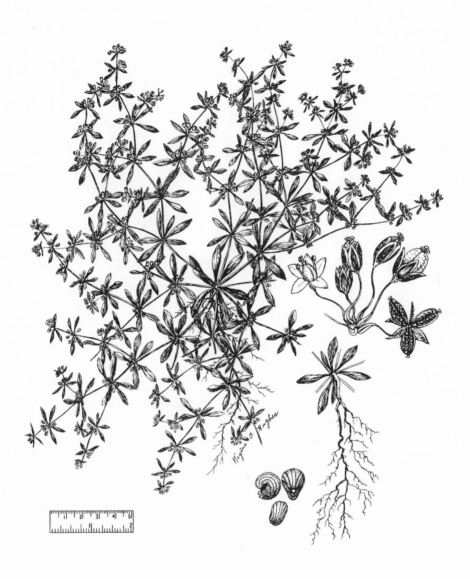

Carpetweed
Mollugo verticillata

Carpetweed
Mollugo verticillata L.

Carpetweed Family
Aizoaceae

EARMARKS. Plant mat-forming; leaves whorled, 5-6 per node; flowers whitish green.

ORIGIN. Tropical America and Africa.

LIFE CYCLE. Summer annual.

STEMS. Branched and smooth; they spread in all directions from the roots and form mats up to at least 0.3 m across.

LEAVES. Simple, entire, rounded at the apex, and 1-2.5 cm long.

FLOWERS. Tiny, stalked, and in groups of 2-5 in umbel-like clusters in the leaf axils; each has 5 sepals, 3 stamens, and 1 pistil. Blooms May through September.

FRUITS. Capsules with many minute, brownish red, kidney-shaped, glossy seeds about 0.5 mm long.

DISTRIBUTION. Roadsides, turf, waste places, gardens, and fallow and cultivated fields throughout the state.

This delicate, mat-forming weed, also known as *indian chickweed*, is used as a potherb by certain Indian tribes.

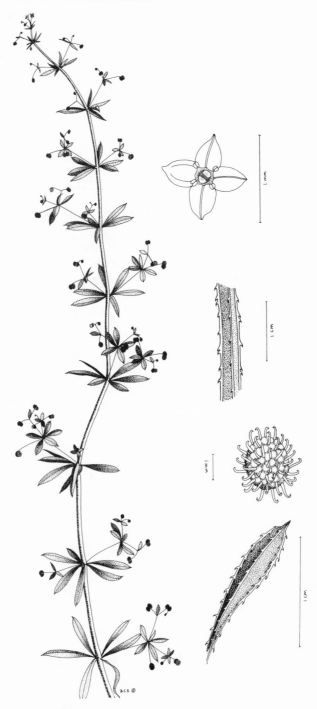

Catchweed Bedstraw
Galium aparine

Catchweed Bedstraw

Galium aparine L.

Madder Family

Rubiaceae

EARMARKS. Stems angled, with backward-pointing hooks; leaves whorled, entire; flowers white, tiny, stalked.

ORIGIN. United States and Eurasia.

LIFE CYCLE. Winter annual.

STEMS. Weak, sprawling, 4-angled, and 6-15 dm tall.

LEAVES. In well-separated groups of 6-8; they are narrow, simple, entire, 1-nerved, bristly, and 1.5-7 cm long.

FLOWERS. Single or in clusters of 2-3 in the leaf axils; each has 4 petals. Blooms May through July.

FRUITS. Yellowish brown to grey-brown, 2-3 mm wide, and covered with hooked prickles and warts.

DISTRIBUTION. Gardens, waste places, rich moist woods, meadows, pastures, fencerows, and fallow and cultivated fields throughout the state.

Galium means "milk." This plant was used in the early days to curdle milk for making cheese, and because the prickly stems cling together, they have been used also to make coarse sieves for straining milk.

An old tale is that one of the species in this genus was found in the hay on which the Virgin Mary rested, hence the name *bedstraw.*

The weed is also called *goosegrass.* It is greatly favored by geese and may be collected for poultry feed.

Mouseearcress

Mustard Family

Arabidopsis thaliana (L.) Heynh.

Brassicaceae

EARMARKS.   Leaves mostly in a basal rosette; flowers white to pinkish, tiny; fruits linear, slightly curved.

ORIGIN.   Europe.

LIFE CYCLE.   Winter annual.

STEMS.   Slender, erect, usually branched near the base, and 5-50 cm tall.

LEAVES.   Variable; the lower ones are oblong to obovate, entire or slightly toothed, and 1-5 cm long; the upper ones are smaller, narrow, and stalkless.

FLOWERS.   In elongated clusters; each has 4 petals 2-4 mm long, which extend beyond the 4 sepals. Blooms March through May.

FRUITS.   Smooth, slender, 1-1.5 cm long, and many-seeded, Borne on threadlike, ascending stalks.

DISTRIBUTION.   Roadsides, turf, gardens, wooded slopes, waste places, and fallow and cultivated fields throughout the state.

The species name commemorates Johann Thal, who wrote about the plant in the sixteenth century.

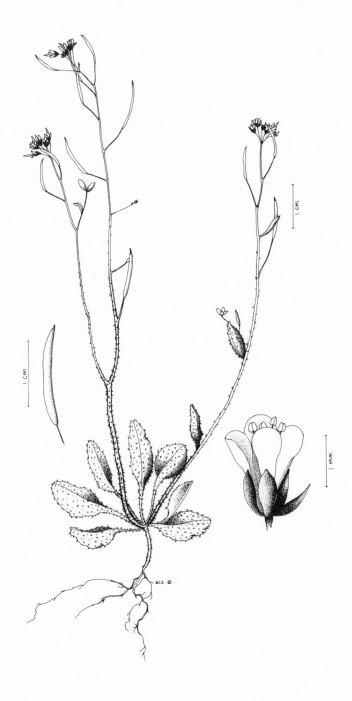

Mouseearcress
Arabidopsis thaliana

Shepherdspurse
Capsella bursa-pastoris (L.) Medic.

Mustard Family

Brassicaceae

EARMARKS. Leaves mostly basal, divided or lobed; flowers white, tiny; seed pods triangular or heart-shaped.

ORIGIN. Europe.

LIFE CYCLE. Winter annual.

STEMS. Erect, sparingly branched, and up to 6 cm long.

LEAVES. Variable; the lower ones, in basal rosettes, are either divided into cleft segments or slightly lobed; the stem leaves are few, alternate, arrowhead-shaped, stalkless, and 5-10 cm long.

FLOWERS. In clusters on slender stalks; each has 4 sepals and 4 petals. Blooms March until frost.

FRUITS. Seed pods containing small, orangish brown, oblong seeds 0.8-1.2 mm long.

DISTRIBUTION. Roadsides, turf, gardens, pastures, waste places, and fallow and cultivated fields throughout the state.

The common name comes from the resemblance of the flat seed pods to an old-fashioned change purse. The dried leaves and fruit pods, which are slightly peppery in taste, are used for seasoning soups and salads.

In the Middle Ages, shepherdspurse was a "blood herb." It was said to stop the flow of blood anywhere on the body, even if the plant was only held in the hand. Today, herbalists use it for its supposed ability to heal open wounds and haemorrhages.

Shepherdspurse
Capsella bursa-pastoris

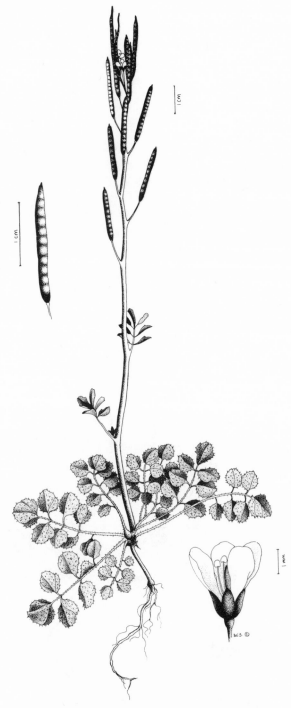

Hairy Bittercress
Cardamine hirsuta

Hairy Bittercress
Cardamine hirsuta L.

Mustard Family
Brassicaceae

EARMARKS. Leaves mostly basal and lobed, stalks hairy at base; flowers white, tiny; seed pods slender, ascending.

ORIGIN. Europe.

LIFE CYCLE. Winter annual.

STEMS. One to several, smooth, erect, and up to 4 dm tall.

LEAVES. In basal rosettes with 1-3 pairs of rounded, lobed leaflets with the terminal lobe the largest; the few smaller, alternate stem leaves have narrow segments; leaf stalks and upper surfaces of blades are hairy.

FLOWERS. In clusters; each has 4 sepals and 4 petals 2-3 mm long. Blooms March through April.

FRUITS. Narrow seed pods 1.5-2.5 cm long.

DISTRIBUTION. Roadsides, turf, gardens, disturbed sites, and fallow and cultivated fields throughout the state.

The generic name is derived from the Greek word *kardamon*, which refers to a plant in the mustard family.

Spring Whitlowgrass
Draba verna L.

Mustard Family
Brassicaceae

EARMARKS. Plant delicate, with basal leaves only; flowers white; seed pods small, on threadlike stalks.

ORIGIN. Europe.

LIFE CYCLE. Winter annual.

STEMS. Ascending, threadlike, naked, and up to 13 cm tall.

LEAVES. Oblanceolate or spatulate, green- or purple-tinged, and up to 1.5 cm long.

FLOWERS. Produced in clusters at the tips of the stems; each is tiny and has 4 sepals and 4 deeply cleft petals. Blooms March through early May.

FRUITS. Oblong to elliptic, smooth pods 4-10 mm long; each contains as many as 60 minute, orange-brown seeds notched at the base and 0.7 mm long.

DISTRIBUTION. Pastures, turf, gravelly soils, and fallow and cultivated fields throughout the state.

This plant has been used to treat Whitlow disease, a hoof inflammation.

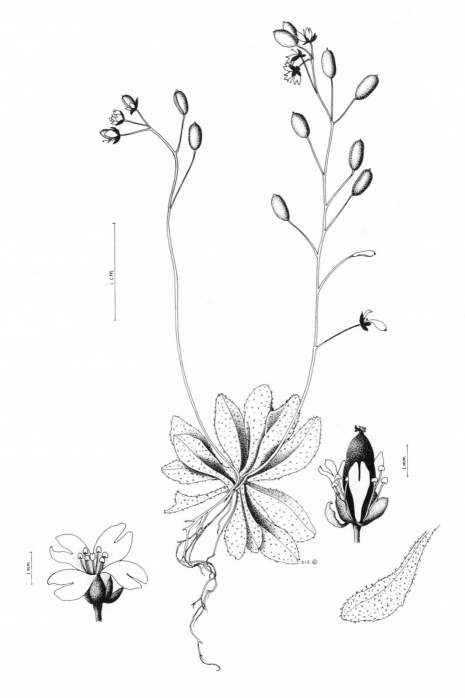

Spring Whitlowgrass
Draba verna

Sibara
Sibara virginica (L.) Rollins

Mustard Family
Brassicaceae

EARMARKS. Leaves deeply divided with a heel-like projection at the base of each segment; flowers white, tiny; fruit pods slender, on threadlike, ascending stalks.

ORIGIN. United States.

LIFE CYCLE. Winter annual.

STEMS. Loosely branched, ascending or decumbent, and 1-4 dm tall.

LEAVES. Variable; basal leaves are oblong, deeply divided with oblong or linear divisions, and with the terminal lobe largest; stem leaves are similar except for the uppermost which are narrow and entire.

FLOWERS. Produced in clusters; each has 4 sepals and 4 petals 1.5-3 mm long. Blooms March through early May.

FRUITS. Broadly linear, flattish, stiff seedpods 2-2.5 mm long; each pod contains several winged seeds 1.5 mm long.

DISTRIBUTION. Gardens, turf, waste places, rocky sites, and fallow and cultivated fields throughout the state.

This small, slender weed is often overlooked in early spring. It is closely related to the bittercresses (*Cardamine*) and the rock-cresses (*Arabis*).

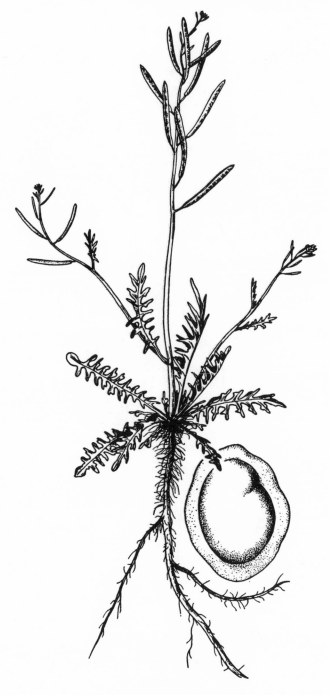

Sibara
Sibara virginica

Star-of-Bethlehem
Ornithogalum umbellatum

Star-of-Bethlehem
Ornithogalum umbellatum L.

Lily Family
Liliaceae

EARMARKS.   Plant poisonous; leaves basal, grasslike; flowers white, star-shaped, with a green band on the back of each sepal and petal.

ORIGIN.   Europe.

LIFE CYCLE.   Perennial herb.

STEMS.   In clumps that arise from a bulb and are 1-3 dm tall.

LEAVES.   Slightly fleshy, narrow, with a pale midrib, and as long as the stem.

FLOWERS.   In flat-topped clusters; they open only in bright sunshine; each has 3 sepals, 3 petals, and 6 yellow stamens. Blooms April through May.

FRUITS.   Capsules, each with several black, roundish, rough seeds about 1.5 mm long.

DISTRIBUTION.   Roadsides, turf, gardens, fields, and pastures throughout the state.

Also called *snowdrops* and *nap-at-noon*, this ornamental plant was introduced from Europe and has escaped to become a troublesome weed. It reproduces mostly by bulbs and can easily be confused with wild garlic. However, the bulbs of the star-of-bethlehem do not smell of onion or garlic.

Cattle and other livestock can be poisoned by eating any part of the plant, either fresh or dried in hay.

Yellow Flowers

Poison Ivy
Rhus radicans L.

Cashew Family
Anacardiaceae

EARMARKS. Plant woody, erect or viney; leaves alternate, long-petioled, with 3 leaflets, the middle leaflet long-stalked; flowers yellowish green.

ORIGIN. United States.

LIFE CYCLE. Perennial woody vine or shrub.

STEMS. Erect or viney; when climbing, they are supported by aerial roots.

LEAVES. Composed of 3 leaflets that are 5-10 cm long; leaflet edges are entire, toothed, or lobed; the surfaces are smooth or hairy and dull or shiny; the apex tapers to a point.

FLOWERS. In open, slender, axillary clusters up to 1 dm long. Blooms June through July.

FRUITS. Whitish-greenish-yellowish berries 3-4 mm wide, each with a striped, 1-seeded stone.

DISTRIBUTION. Roadsides, railroad embankments, riverbanks, rocky woods, thickets, waste places, vacant lots, fencerows, and pastures throughout the state.

Some people are so sensitive to poison ivy that the slightest contact will cause a severe reaction, whereas others can handle it with little or no adverse effect.

The plant produces a nonvolatile oil. When this is absorbed by the human skin itchy blisters develop, often followed by swelling of the affected surface.

An American Indian remedy consists of squeezing the sticky juice of jewelweed or touch-me-not (*Impatiens biflora* Willd., or *Impatiens pallida* Nutt.) on affected areas until they heal.

Poison Ivy
Rhus radicans

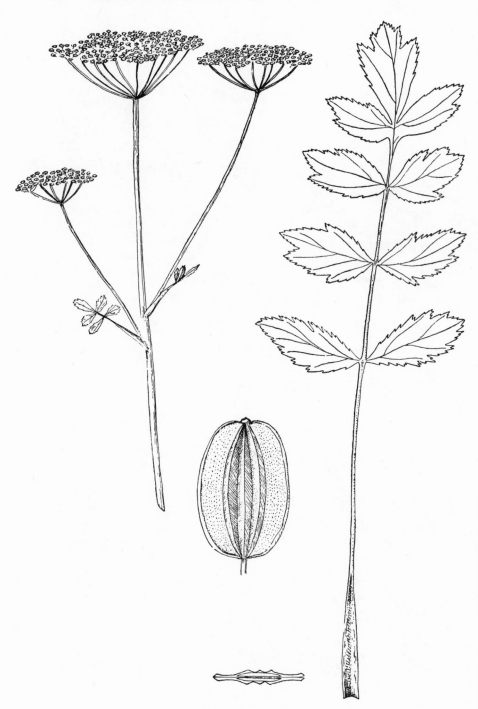

Wild Parsnip
Pastinaca sativa

Wild Parsnip
Pastinaca sativa L.

Parsley Family
Apiaceae

EARMARKS. Leaves alternate, pinnate; flowers yellow, tiny, in umbels.

ORIGIN. Europe.

LIFE CYCLE. Monocarpic perennial.

STEMS. Coarse, branching, grooved, hollow, and up to 1.5 m tall.

LEAVES. Divided into 5-15 oblong to ovate, toothed leaflets 5-11 cm long; the lower leaves are long-stalked, and the upper ones are short-stalked.

FLOWERS. In large umbels at the stem tips; the terminal umbel is soon surpassed by the lateral ones. Blooms June through July.

FRUITS. Straw-colored, flat, elliptic to obovate, seedlike, and 5-7 mm long.

DISTRIBUTION. Roadsides, railroad embankments, waste places, moist meadows, thickets, clearcuts, gardens, fencerows, and pastures throughout the state.

Parsnip is a well-known culinary herb introduced into the United States from Europe. In the wild, the thick, fleshy roots of wild parsnip are poisonous. The cultivated parsnip never develops toxicity even if it has escaped from the home garden.

Photosensitization develops in people with sensitive skin who touch the leaves or stems of wild or cultivated parsnip. After contact with the plant and exposure to sunlight, a rash appears which can be severe.

Annual Wormwood

Artemisia annua L.

Composite Family

Asteraceae

EARMARKS. Plant sweet-smelling; leaves alternate, fernlike, yellowish green; flower heads yellowish green, nodding, in loosely spreading clusters.

ORIGIN. Eurasia.

LIFE CYCLE. Summer annual.

STEMS. Smooth, bushy-branched, and 6-12 dm tall.

LEAVES. Finely divided 2-3 times into narrow segments; the lower leaves are long-stalked; the upper ones are stalkless.

FLOWER HEADS. Small and roundish; the base of each flower head is enclosed by a few, tiny, greenish bracts. Blooms August through October.

FRUITS. Yellow, oval, and obscurely nerved, seedlike achenes.

DISTRIBUTION. Roadsides, gardens, fields, woodland thickets, waste places, and barnyards throughout the state.

The genus *Artemisia* was named either after a Carian princess or after the Greek Goddess Diana, who presided over the health of women.

Wormwoods are popular in landscaping as border plants because their aromatic nature imparts fragrance to the garden. Some herb growers cultivate annual wormwood for making potpourris and scented wreaths.

X ½

Annual Wormwood
Artemisia annua

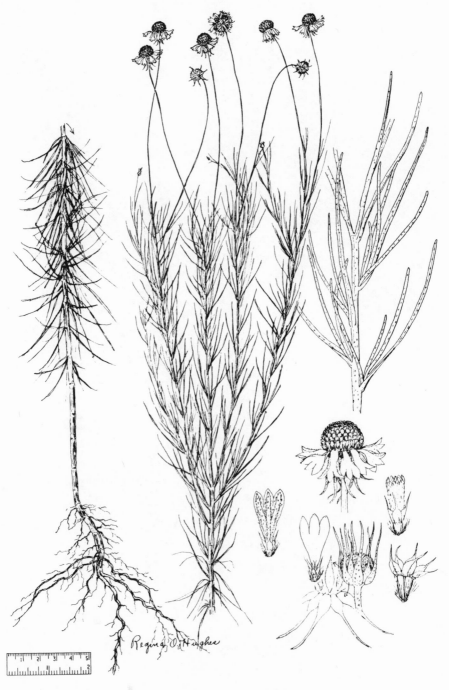

Bitter Sneezeweed
Helenium amarum

Bitter Sneezeweed

Helenium amarum (Raf.) H. Rock

Composite Family

Asteraceae

EARMARKS. Leaves alternate, narrow to threadlike, and crowded on the stem; flower heads bright yellow.

ORIGIN. Southwestern United States.

LIFE CYCLE. Winter annual.

STEMS. Erect and covered with small, yellow-dotted glands; they are branched at the tip and 1-8 dm tall.

LEAVES. Smooth, granular-dotted, and 1.5-8 cm long.

FLOWER HEADS. Rounded, 1.5-3.5 cm wide, and produced on long stalks at the tips of the stems; the base of each flower head is enclosed by many inconspicuous bracts. Blooms July through September.

FRUITS. Hairy, seedlike achenes 1-1.5 mm long that taper to a narrow base; the apex has ovate scales and is bristle-tipped.

DISTRIBUTION. Roadsides, waste places in dry, open ground, and old feed lots throughout the western and southwestern parts of the state. Bitter sneezeweed is especially common in pastures, where severe infestations can occur.

This plant is known also as *yellow dogfennel*. It contains a narcotic that has poisoned grazing horses, mules, sheep, and cattle. Although most livestock avoid these plants, poisoning usually occurs in late summer when the plants are in bloom.

Prickly Lettuce

Composite Family

Lactuca serriola L.

Asteraceae

[Syn. *Lactuca scariola* L.]

EARMARKS. Leaves arrowhead-shaped, prickly, clasping the stem; flower heads yellow, dandelionlike but small.

ORIGIN. Europe.

LIFE CYCLE. Winter annual.

STEMS. Erect, green or yellowish, and up to 15 dm tall.

LEAVES. Alternate; the lower ones are 6-30 cm long and deeply or shallowly lobed with one to several lobes on each side; the upper ones are small and narrow; all leaves have a distinct midrib beneath and prickly margins.

FLOWER HEADS. Produced in an open, diffuse inflorescence with about 13-24 ray flowers per head; the base of each head is enclosed by many greenish bracts. Blooms July through September.

FRUITS. Black to grey seedlike achenes, each with a long beak crowned with a tuft of white hairs at the tip.

DISTRIBUTION. Roadsides, waste places, gardens, fence-rows, pastures, vacant lots, orchards, and fallow and cultivated fields throughout the state.

Prickly lettuce contains more vitamin A than spinach and a large quantity of vitamin C.

The latex can cause dermatitis in people with sensitive skin.

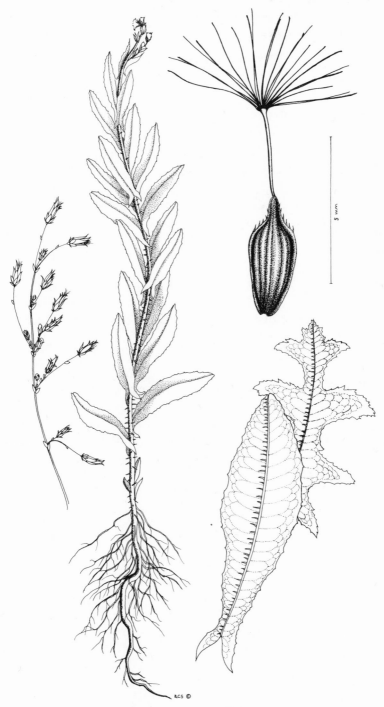

Prickly Lettuce
Lactuca serriola

Pineappleweed

Composite Family

Matricaria matricarioides (Less.)   Asteraceae
C.L. Porter

EARMARKS. Plants smell like pineapple; leaves alternate, fernlike; flower heads yellowish green, cone-shaped.

ORIGIN. Pacific coast and spreading eastward.

LIFE CYCLE. Summer annual.

STEMS. Erect or spreading, branched, smooth, and 1-4 dm high.

LEAVES. Very finely divided.

FLOWER HEADS. Numerous; they are solitary on short stalks at the tops of the stems; the base of each flower head is enclosed by many greenish bracts. Blooms June through August.

FRUITS. Yellowish grey, seedlike achenes, each 1-1.5 mm long, obovate to oblong, and 3- to 5-ribbed, and having a small tubercle in the middle.

DISTRIBUTION. Roadsides, waste places, trodden paths, turf, gardens, and pastures throughout the state.

This plant imparts an unmistakable fragrance of pineapple as soon as the leaves or flowers are crushed or bruised. The Blackfoot Indians gathered and dried the small, cone-shaped flower heads and used them to make perfume and insect repellent.

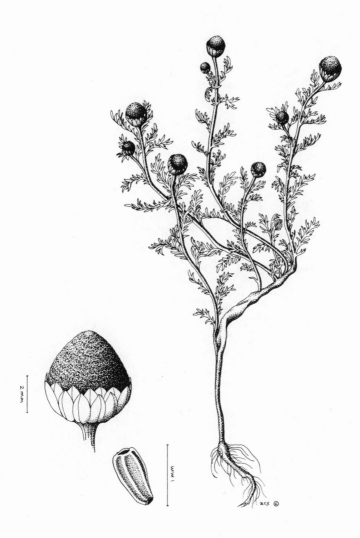

Pineappleweed
Matricaria matricarioides

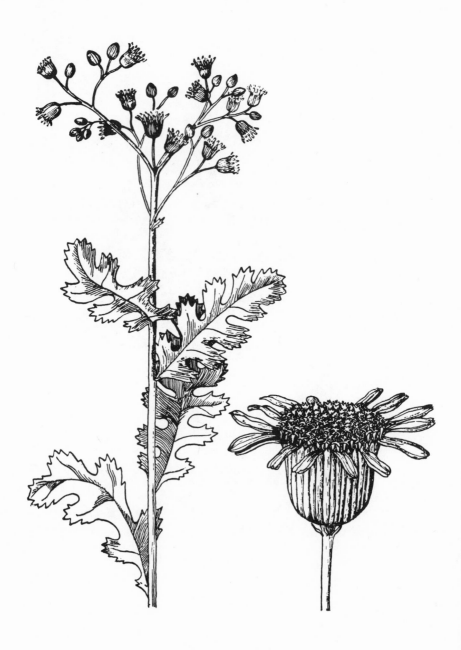

Cressleaf Groundsel
Senecio glabellus

Cresnleaf Groundsel

Senecio glabellus Poir.

Composite Family

Asteraceae

EARMARKS. Plant succulent with hollow stems; leaves alternate, deeply divided; flower heads bright yellow, daisylike.

ORIGIN. United States.

LIFE CYCLE. Biennial.

STEMS. Succulent, smooth, ridged, hollow, and up to 1 m tall.

LEAVES. Variable; the basal and lower leaves, which are up to 20 cm long, are deeply divided and have each a large, rounded, terminal lobe; the stem leaves are similar but diminish in size upward.

FLOWER HEADS. Small and produced in clusters at the tips of the slender stems; the base of each flower head is enclosed by long, tapering green bracts. Blooms April through May.

FRUITS. Small, smooth to slightly hairy, seedlike achenes.

DISTRIBUTION. Wet woods, swamps, streambanks, pastures, roadsides, and fallow and cultivated fields throughout the western half of the state, especially on rich riverbottom soils. The plant is occasionally found in the eastern and northern parts of the state.

This plant is a member of one of the largest genera of plants. The generic name *Senecio* comes from the Latin *senex*, which means "old man," an allusion to the white hairs on the apex of the fruit.

The common name is from the Anglo-Saxon *groundeswelge*, meaning "ground-swallower" and referring to the spreading habit of the plant.

Spiny Sowthistle
Sonchus asper

Spiny Sowthistle
Sonchus asper (L.) Hill

Composite Family
Asteraceae

EARMARKS. Leaves alternate with clasping, heart-shaped bases; flower heads pale yellow, dandelionlike.

ORIGIN. Western Asia, northern Africa, and Europe.

LIFE CYCLE. Summer annual.

STEMS. Branched or single, often reddish, leafy, and 3-10 dm tall.

LEAVES. Obovate to oblanceolate, entire to many-lobed, and prickly margined; they become progressively smaller upward.

FLOWER HEADS. Each is 1.2-2.5 mm wide, arranged in open clusters, the base enclosed by long, green bracts. Blooms early June through October.

FRUITS. Light brown, ribbed, seedlike achenes 2-3 mm long, with winged margins.

DISTRIBUTION. Roadsides, railroad embankments, waste places, gardens, fencerows, open meadows, and fallow and cultivated fields throughout the state.

SIMILAR SPECIES. Annual sowthistle, *Sonchus oleraceus* L., a summer annual, has leaves that are deeply lobed into 1-3 segments on each side, with the top lobe broadly triangular. The brown to olive seedlike achenes have less prominent ribs but more transverse markings and grow to 1 mm in length.

The sowthistles have a milky juice and a bitter taste similar to that of dandelion and chicory.

In parts of Europe, the young leaves are used as a potherb or salad.

Western Salsify   Composite Family

Tragopogon dubius Scop.   Asteraceae
[Syn. *Tragopogon major* Jacq.]

EARMARKS.   Plant has milky sap; leaves alternate, grasslike; flower heads yellow, dandelionlike.

ORIGIN.   Europe.

LIFE CYCLE.   Biennial.

STEMS.   Swollen below the flower heads; they are coarse, light green, and 15-60 cm tall.

LEAVES.   Long, narrow, and entire; each clasps the stem at the base and is 10-30 cm long.

FLOWER HEADS.   Solitary, 2-5 cm wide, and produced at the tips of the branches; the narrow bracts at the base of each flower head are longer than the flowers. Blooms May through early July.

FRUITS.   Long, ridged, seedlike achenes 2.5-3.5 mm long, each narrowing into a slender beak with feathery bristles attached at the tip; the head of achenes is a conspicuous, fluffy ball.

DISTRIBUTION.   Roadsides, pastures, fields, and waste places throughout the state.

The flower heads open in the morning, close by noon, and are soon replaced by the showy, fluffy fruit clusters.

Western Salsify
Tragopogon dubius

Yellow Rocket
Barbarea vulgaris

Yellow Rocket
Barbarea vulgaris R. Br.

Mustard Family
Brassicaceae

EARMARKS. Leaves alternate; flowers bright yellow; seed pods slender, slightly curved.

ORIGIN. Europe.

LIFE CYCLE. Biennial or winter annual.

STEMS. Numerous, ridged, often branched at the top, and 2-9 dm tall.

LEAVES. Variable; the basal ones have a large terminal lobe and 1-4 smaller, lateral lobes; the upper leaves are progressively shorter-stalked and have fewer lobes; the uppermost leaves are clasping and entire or toothed.

FLOWERS. In elongated clusters; each has 4 sepals and 4 petals arranged in the form of a cross, and 6 stamens (4 long and 2 short). Blooms April through June.

FRUITS. Seed pods 1.5 mm wide, squarish in cross-section, beaked, and borne on stalks 3-6 mm long.

DISTRIBUTION. Roadsides, waste places, pastures, bottomlands in rich alluvial soils, and fallow and cultivated fields throughout the state.

This bright-yellow-flowered weed commemorates St. Barbara of the fourth century. It was introduced into North America before 1800. Like many members of the mustard family, the leaves and new stems can be boiled like spinach or used as a salad green. Because it yields nectar and pollen it is visited by bees in great numbers.

Hedge Mustard

Sisymbrium officinale (L.) Scop.
var. *leiocarpum* DC.

Mustard Family

Brassicaceae

EARMARKS.   Leaves alternate, deeply lobed; flowers yellow, tiny; fruit pods narrow and sharp-pointed.

ORIGIN.   Europe.

LIFE CYCLE.   Winter annual.

STEMS.   Stiff, erect, branched, and up to 1.2 m tall.

LEAVES.   Pale green and variable; the lower ones are pinnately lobed and each has a large terminal lobe with smaller lateral lobes that are irregularly toothed; the upper ones are smaller, arrow-shaped, and narrow.

FLOWERS.   Produced in elongated clusters in the leaf axils and branch tips; they are 4-petalled and about 3 mm long. Blooms late April through August.

FRUITS.   Awl-shaped seed pods that lie close against the branches; they are 1-2 cm long and contain several small, greenish brown seeds about 1.5 mm long.

DISTRIBUTION.   Roadsides, gardens, fields, waste places, and fallow and cultivated fields throughout the state.

Rondelet, a well-respected sixteenth-century physician and naturalist, boasted that he had cured himself by using this herb after losing his voice, and proclaimed it a valuable medicine for treating diseases of the chest, lungs, and throat.

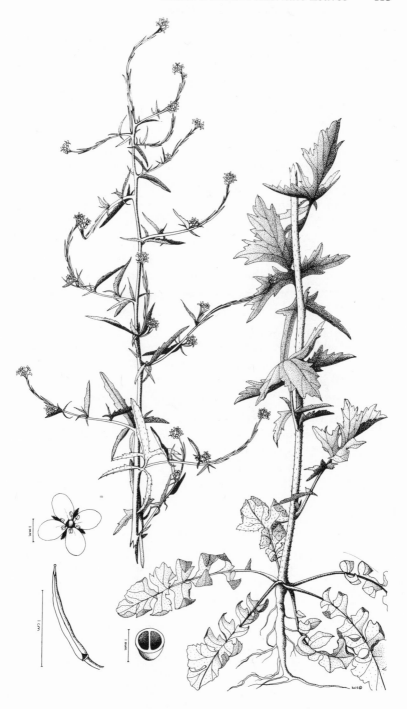

Hedge Mustard
Sisymbrium officinale var. *leiocarpum*

Partridgepea

Legume Family

Cassia fasciculata Michx.

Fabaceae

EARMARKS. Leaves alternate, pinnately compound; flowers bright yellow, with long, dark brown stamens.

ORIGIN. United States.

LIFE CYCLE. Summer annual.

STEMS. Erect and hairy; they grow from 3-9 cm tall.

LEAVES. Pinnately compound, with 5-17 pairs of linear-oblong leaflets each pointed at the tip; a single, small, rounded, dark gland is produced on the leaf stalk.

FLOWERS. Produced on slender stalks in the leaf axils; each has 5 sepals, 5 irregularly shaped petals 1-2 cm long, and 10 unequal stamens. Blooms July through August.

FRUITS. Long, narrow, flat pods that contain several black seeds each with rows of pits on the surface.

DISTRIBUTION. Most abundant in open sandy areas, woodland clearings, cultivated fields, and roadsides in the Knobs and the western part of the state. It is uncommon in the Bluegrass Region.

SIMILAR SPECIES. Sicklepod, *Senna obtusifolia* L., a summer annual, has pale yellow flowers, broad, obovate leaflets, and long, slender, curved pods. It is found in a few scattered locations in western, southern, and eastern Kentucky. It is most common in the western part of the state, especially in riverbottom soils in the Purchase Area.

Partridgepea is considered a pioneer species and often forms dense stands on infertile, disturbed sites where other plants cannot grow.

The showy yellow flowers are without nectar. However, the petiolar glands just below the first pair of leaflets supply nectar to several kinds of short-tongued bees and a variety of flies and ants.

Partridgepea
Cassia fasciculata

Black Medic
Medicago lupulina L.

Legume Family
Fabaceae

EARMARKS.   Plant spreading; leaves alternate, divided into 3 leaflets; flowers small, yellow.

ORIGIN.   Eurasia.

LIFE CYCLE.   Winter annual or biennial.

STEMS.   Rough, hairy, branched at the base, and up to 6 m long.

LEAVES.   Stalked, with 3 wedge-shaped leaflets that are toothed at the tip; the terminal one is stalked; the stipules are ovate-lanceolate and hairy.

FLOWERS.   In small, rounded clusters 3-4 mm long; each has 5 sepals, 5 petals, and 10 stamens. Blooms May through October.

FRUITS.   Coiled, 1-seeded, kidney-shaped pods that turn black at maturity; the yellowish green, oval to kidney-shaped seed is 1.5-2 mm long.

DISTRIBUTION.   Roadsides, turf, gardens, meadows, and fallow and cultivated fields throughout the state.

Species within the genus *Medicago* are believed to have originated in Media, now part of Iran.

Black medic was introduced into North America as a forage crop. It has become a valuable addition to pasturage in the higher mountain ranges of the western United States. Because of its superiority and adaptability to various climates and soils, the plant is also called *nonesuch*, meaning that no other plant is like it. It has escaped, however, and become a troublesome weed throughout its range.

Black Medic

Medicago lupulina

Hemp Sesbania
Sesbania exaltata

Hemp Sesbania

Sesbania exaltata (Raf.) Rydb.
ex A.W. Hill
[Syn. *Sesbania macrocarpa* Muhl.]

Legume Family
Fabaceae

EARMARKS.   Leaves alternate, pinnately compound; flowers pale yellow with purple flecks, pealike.

ORIGIN.   United States.

LIFE CYCLE.   Summer annual.

STEMS.   Smooth, branched, somewhat woody, and up to 3 m tall.

LEAVES.   Pinnately compound with 12-70 pairs of narrowly oblong leaflets.

FLOWERS.   Produced in clusters from the leaf axils. Blooms July through September.

FRUITS.   Distinctly curved pods that are sharply pointed at the apex and about 2 dm long; they contain greyish brown to reddish brown, mottled seeds that are oblong to broadly rounded at both ends.

DISTRIBUTION.   Roadsides, low moist ground, thickets, and cultivated fields. Most common in riverbottom soils in the Purchase Area; rare elsewhere.

Hemp sesbania is a troublesome weed in rice fields in the southern United States. It is spreading northward and has recently become a serious problem in soybean fields in southwestern Kentucky.

Large Hop Clover
Trifolium campestre

Large Hop Clover

Trifolium campestre Schreb.
[Syn. *Trifolium procumbens* L.]

Legume Family
Fabaceae

EARMARKS. Leaves alternate with 3 leaflets; flower clusters yellow.

ORIGIN. Europe.

LIFE CYCLE. Winter annual.

STEMS. Hairy, branched, and 1-2 dm long.

LEAVES. Oblong-obovate, slightly toothed, and 8-15 mm long; the middle leaflet is on a short, jointed stalk.

FLOWERS. In dense, rounded clusters with 20 or more flowers. Blooms May through July.

FRUITS. Pods 1-1.5 mm long, with one to a few yellowish orange seeds.

DISTRIBUTION. Turf, gardens, old fields, pastures, gravelly waste places, and fallow and cultivated fields throughout the state.

SIMILAR SPECIES. Small hop clover, *Trifolium dubium* Sibth., a winter annual, has 5-15 yellow flowers in small, rounded clusters 5-10 mm long. It is common throughout the state.

The word *clover* comes from the Anglo-Saxon *cloefer*, which means "club" and refers to the three-knotted club belonging to Hercules.

Clover has long been an omen of good luck, especially the four-leafed clover.

The hop clovers may be grown as forage crops.

Hophornbeam Copperleaf
Acalypha ostryaefolia

Hophornbeam Copperleaf

Acalypha ostryaefolia Riddell

Spurge Family

Euphorbiaceae

EARMARKS. Leaves alternate, heart-shaped, toothed; flower parts indistinguishable, yellowish green, produced in clusters; floral bracts lobed to the middle.

ORIGIN. West Indies.

LIFE CYCLE. Summer annual.

STEMS. Branched above, finely hairy, pale green, and up to 8 dm tall.

LEAVES. Long-stalked, drooping, thin, and ovate-oblong with closely toothed margins.

FLOWERS. Small, growing in separate male and female clusters; the female clusters are mostly terminal, 3-8 cm long; the male clusters are short and in the leaf axils. Blooms July through September.

FRUITS. Three-lobed capsules with soft, greenish projections and 3 light grey, wrinkled seeds about 2 mm long.

DISTRIBUTION. Roadsides, waste places, thickets, and fallow and cultivated fields throughout the state.

SIMILAR SPECIES. There are two other summer annual *Acalypha* species that are common. Rhombic copperleaf, *Acalypha rhomboidea* Raf., has ovate to rhombic leaves, and bracts that are 5- to 7-lobed and reminiscent of outstretched hands. Virginia copperleaf, *Acalypha virginica* L., has narrower, lanceolate leaves, and bracts that are 9- to 15-lobed.

The plants of this group are also called *waxballs* because of the waxy balls of pollen that are on the stamens when the plant is in full bloom.

Prickly Sida

Mallow Family

Sida spinosa L.

Malvaceae

EARMARKS. Leaves alternate, each with a soft, spinelike projection at the leaf base; flowers pale yellow.

ORIGIN. The tropics.

LIFE CYCLE. Summer annual.

STEMS. Erect, much-branched, hairy, and 2-5 dm tall.

LEAVES. Simple, lanceolate to ovate, toothed, and 1-5 cm long.

FLOWERS. Single or in clusters in the leaf axils; each is small and stalked and has 5 sepals, 5 petals, numerous stamens, and 1 pistil. Blooms June through September.

FRUITS. Round capsules made up of 5 segments that split at the top into 2 beaks; they contain brownish, ovate, 3-angled seeds.

DISTRIBUTION. Roadsides, gardens, waste places, barnyards, and fallow and cultivated fields throughout the state.

In tropical America, a decoction of the plant is thought to be valuable in treating children's sores.

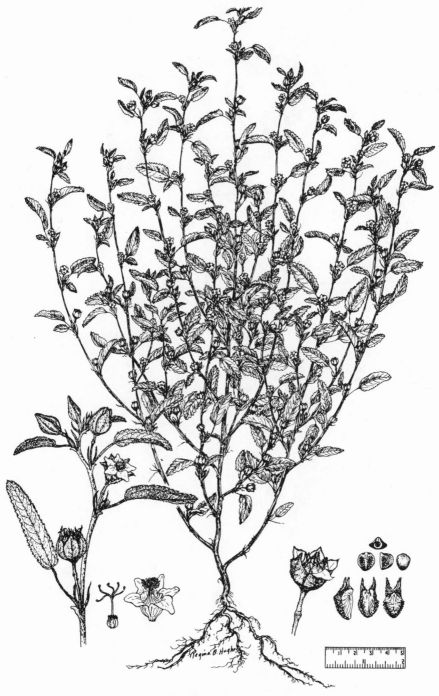

Prickly Sida
Sida spinosa

Creeping Waterprimrose
Ludwigia peploides

Creeping Waterprimrose

Ludwigia peploides (HBK) Raven
[Syn. *Jussiaea repens* L.
var. *glabrescens* Ktze.]

Evening Primrose
Family
Onagraceae

EARMARKS.   Plant aquatic; leaves alternate, floating; flowers bright yellow.

ORIGIN.   Southcentral United States.

LIFE CYCLE.   Perennial herb.

STEMS.   Creeping or floating, simple or forked, often ascending at the tips, and smooth to slightly hairy.

LEAVES.   Long-stalked, smooth, oblong-lanceolate to obovate, and 3-9 cm long.

FLOWERS.   Produced in the leaf axils; each has 5 green sepals, 5 petals 10-15 mm long, 10 stamens, and 1 pistil with a 5-lobed stigma. Blooms June through August.

FRUITS.   Slender, cylindrical capsules 3-5 cm long; seeds are in 5 vertical rows, each row in its own compartment.

DISTRIBUTION.   Ponds, lakes, slow-moving streams, and roadside ditches throughout the state.

The genus was named for Christian Gottlieb Ludwig, a professor of botany in Leipzig.

Common Eveningprimrose
Oenothera biennis L.

Eveningprimrose
Family

Onagraceae

EARMARKS. Leaves alternate, simple; flowers bright yellow.

ORIGIN. United States.

LIFE CYCLE. Monocarpic perennial.

STEMS. Stout, erect, hairy, usually unbranched, and up to 1.5 m tall.

LEAVES. Lanceolate to oblong, toothed, sharp-pointed, ascending or spreading, and 1-2 dm long.

FLOWERS. In terminal clusters; each has 4 reflexed sepals, 4 petals 15-25 mm long, 8 stamens, and a style with a cross-shaped stigma. Blooms June through September.

FRUITS. Cylindrical, 4-angled, velvety-hairy capsules 1-4 cm long that contain many reddish brown, small, irregularly shaped seeds.

DISTRIBUTION. Roadsides, fields, pastures, gardens, and waste places throughout the state.

SIMILAR SPECIES. Cutleaf eveningprimrose, *Oenothera laciniata* Hill, a biennial, is branched from the base and has alternate, oblong to lanceolate leaves that are shallowly to deeply lobed or incised. The single yellow flowers are produced in the upper leaf axils. Blooms May through August.

The first year's rosettes, as well as the roots, of the common eveningprimrose are used as greens and considered by some cooks an essential ingredient in making savory dishes.

Common Eveningprimrose
Oenothera biennis

Yellow Woodsorrel
Oxalis stricta

Yellow Woodsorrel
Oxalis stricta L.

Woodsorrel Family
Oxalidaceae

EARMARKS. Plant often mat-forming; leaves alternate, leaflets in groups of 3, notched at the tips; flowers yellow.

ORIGIN. United States.

LIFE CYCLE. Perennial herb.

STEMS. Freely branched and hairy; they root at the lower nodes and grow up to 5 dm long.

LEAVES. Long-stalked, pale to greyish green, and 1-2 cm wide; they have 3 notched, heart-shaped leaflets.

FLOWERS. Solitary or in small clusters at the tips of the stems; each has 5 sepals, 5 petals, 10 stamens, and 5 styles. Blooms April through May and sporadically throughout the fall.

FRUITS. Five-ridged, cylindrical capsules containing several brown, ridged seeds 1-1.3 mm long; the fruit stalks bend backward when mature.

DISTRIBUTION. Roadsides, turf, gardens, barnyards, pastures, waste places, and fallow and cultivated fields throughout the state.

SIMILAR SPECIES. European woodsorrel, *Oxalis europaea* Jordan, a biennial, has green or purplish leaflets; the flower stalks are not bent in fruit.

Children have called this plant *pickles* because the young green fruits and leaves taste sour.

The woodsorrels, sometimes called *sourgrass*, are used as a folk remedy in Europe, Asia, and North America for the treatment of cancer. They yield also an orange dye.

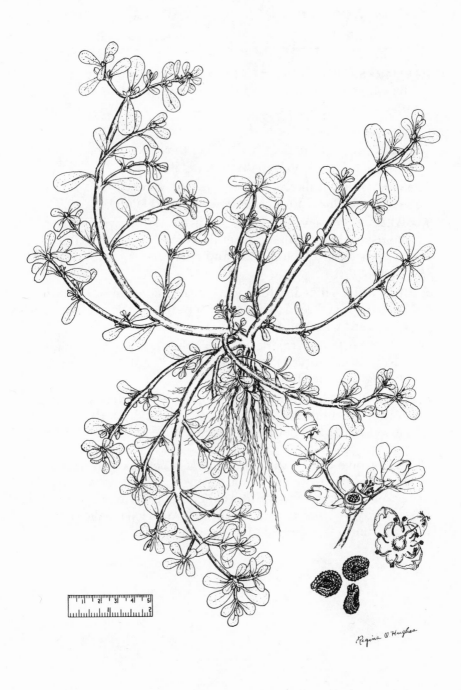

Common Purslane
Portulaca oleracea

Common Purslane
Portulaca oleracea L.

Purslane Family
Portulacaceae

EARMARKS. Plant succulent; leaves alternate or opposite, entire; flowers yellow, small.

ORIGIN. Europe.

LIFE CYCLE. Summer annual.

STEMS. Freely branched, often mat-forming; they are smooth, usually tinged with purple, and up to 5.5 dm long.

LEAVES. Obovate or wedge-shaped, fleshy, and thick; they are often in clusters at the branch tips.

FLOWERS. Solitary in the leaf axils or in clusters at the stem tips; each has 2 sepals, 5 petals, and 7-12 stamens. Blooms June through September.

FRUITS. Rounded capsules, the tops of which come off like lids exposing the black, circular to kidney-shaped seeds. Each seed has a yellow scar at the end and rough bumps on the surface.

DISTRIBUTION. Roadsides, turf, gardens, sidewalk cracks, waste places, and fallow and cultivated fields throughout the state.

Common purslane was present in temperate North America 2,500-3,000 years ago and spread, in part, because it was used by the Indians.

It has been grown as a garden vegetable in Europe and Asia for thousands of years. Today, its fleshy leaves and young stems are still used as salad greens and cooked vegetables.

Long ago, the plant was valued for its supposed power to ward off magic spells cast upon people or their cattle. It was spread around beds as protection from evil spirits, which would visit the sleepers at night.

Smallflower Buttercup
Ranunculus abortivus L.

Buttercup Family
Ranunculaceae

EARMARKS. Plant weak-stemmed; leaves alternate, variable; flowers tiny, yellow.

ORIGIN. United States.

LIFE CYCLE. Biennial.

STEMS. Weak, smooth, forked at the top, and up to 6 dm tall.

LEAVES. Variable; the basal ones are circular or have 3 obovate leaflets; the stem leaves are usually stalkless and are either deeply lobed or divided into 3-5 blunt-tipped, narrow to obovate segments.

FLOWERS. Small, solitary, and produced at the branch tips; each has 5 downward-bent sepals, 5 petals, and many stamens. Blooms April through early June.

FRUITS. Beaked, seedlike achenes 1.5 mm long grouped in compact bunches.

DISTRIBUTION. Roadsides, pastures, moist meadows, gardens, turf, and fallow and cultivated fields throughout the state.

The generic name derives from the Latin name *Rana*, which means "frog" and refers to the aquatic habits of some species. The species name, from the Latin *abortus*, means "miscarriage or incomplete," and alludes to the inconspicuous petals, which give the impression of an incomplete flower.

Smallflower Buttercup
Ranunculus abortivus

Common Mullein
Verbascum thapsus L.

Figwort Family
Scrophulariaceae

EARMARKS. Plant woolly; leaves alternate, entire; flowers bright yellow, circular in outline.

ORIGIN. Eurasia.

LIFE CYCLE. Monocarpic perennial.

STEMS. Stout and woolly, erect, unbranched or occasionally with a few upright branches near the top, and 5-25 dm tall.

LEAVES. Large, thick, and woolly at the base of the plant; Each is oblong, distinctly veined, tapered into a thick base, and 15-24 cm long; the upper stem leaves are narrower and have leaf bases that run down the stem making it appear winged and 4-angled.

FLOWERS. Produced in long, dense, terminal clusters; only a few open at a time to expose the 5 woolly sepals, 5 united petals, and bearded stamens. Blooms June through September.

FRUITS. Round capsules 6 mm wide that contain seeds with wavy ridges and deep grooves.

DISTRIBUTION. Roadsides, railroad embankments, pastures, fencerows, waste places, woodland borders, and clearcuts throughout the state.

This plant is known also as *jacob's staff* or *flannel-leaf.* A folk term was *candlewicks*, so named because the hairs on the leaves were scraped off and used to make candlewicks.

In the fifth and fourth centuries B.C., the flowers were used to make yellow hair dye. A soap made from the ashes of the leaves was said to restore graying hair to its original color.

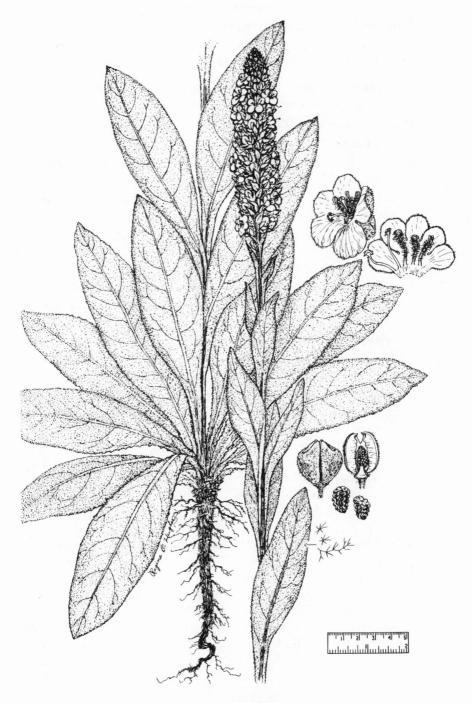

Common Mullein
Verbascum thapsus

Clammy Groundcherry
Physalis heterophylla Nees

Nightshade Family
Solanaceae

EARMARKS. Plant sticky; leaves alternate; flowers dull yellow, each with dark spots in the center.

ORIGIN. United States.

LIFE CYCLE. Perennial herb.

STEMS. Branched, hairy, glandular, ridged, and up to 8 dm tall.

LEAVES. Broadly ovate, 3-8 cm long, simple, hairy, and lopsided at the base.

FLOWERS. Solitary, drooping, and emerging from the leaf axils; each has 5 sepals, 5 petals, and 5 stamens. Blooms June through August.

FRUITS. Round, yellow berries, each surrounded by an inflated calyx and containing many straw-colored, obovate seeds about 2 mm long.

DISTRIBUTION. Roadsides, gardens, old fields, pastures, waste places, and fallow and cultivated fields throughout the state.

SIMILAR SPECIES. Smooth groundcherry, *Physalis subglabrata* Mack. & Bush, a perennial herb, has smooth stems, coarsely toothed, ovate leaves, and yellow flowers with dark centers. Cutleaf groundcherry, *Physalis angulata* L., a summer annual, has smooth stems and alternate, ovate to lanceolate leaves with irregular to nearly entire margins. Flowers yellow and solitary. Found in the western half of the state.

Across the prairie in the United States carbonized seeds of clammy groundcherry dating from 2280 B.C. to 985 A.D. have been found.

The generic name means "plant with bladdery husk"; *heterophylla* means "having leaves of different shapes."

Indian children called the plant *popweed* because they could pop the inflated husks against their foreheads.

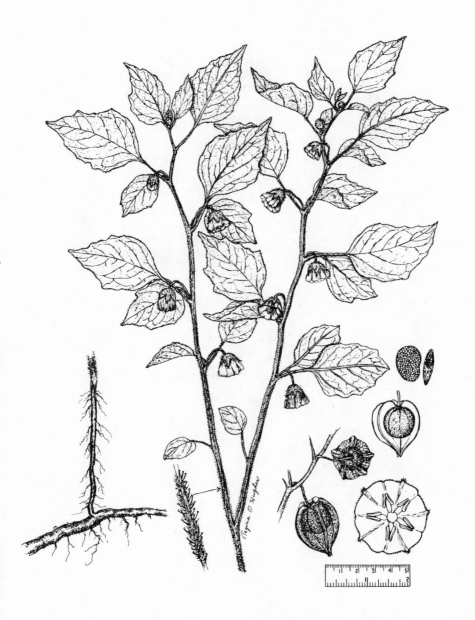

Clammy Groundcherry
Physalis heterophylla

Field Violet
Viola arvensis

Field Violet

Viola arvensis Murr.

Violet Family

Violaceae

EARMARKS. Leaves alternate, toothed; flowers small, yellow with purple-tipped petals.

ORIGIN. Europe.

LIFE CYCLE. Winter annual.

STEMS. Simple to slightly branched, leafy, angled, slightly hairy, and 1-3 dm long.

LEAVES. Variable in shape; the lower stem leaves are circular to ovate and bluntly toothed; the upper ones are oblong to lanceolate and blunt- or sharp-toothed; each stipule is large, leaflike and deeply divided, with the middle lobe enlarged.

FLOWERS. Produced on long slender stalks in the leaf axils; each has 5 narrow, sharp-pointed sepals, 5 petals that are seldom longer than the sepals, and 5 stamens that surround 1 clublike pistil. Blooms April and May, August and September.

FRUITS. Three-valved, rounded capsules that contain many yellow to brown, glossy, obovoid seeds 1 mm long.

DISTRIBUTION. Roadsides, pastures, open meadows, waste places, turf, and fallow and cultivated fields throughout the state.

SIMILAR SPECIES. Field pansy, *Viola rafinesquii* Greene, a winter annual, has stipules with the middle lobes narrow, long, and entire; the whitish to pale purple petals are longer than the sepals.

In the eastern United States there are over 50 different species of violets, some of which are difficult to identify because they can easily hybridize.

It is said that the English settlers in America were delighted to see so many violets. They used them as an ingredient in cosmetics and sweet waters. The herb, bound to the forehead, is said to induce sleep.

Bearded Beggarticks
Bidens aristosa (Michx.) Britt.

Composite Family
Asteraceae

EARMARKS. Leaves opposite or whorled; flower heads bright yellow, daisylike; fruits with barbed bristles.

ORIGIN. United States.

LIFE CYCLE. Summer annual.

STEMS. Smooth to slightly hairy and 3-15 cm tall.

LEAVES. Deeply divided into many lanceolate or linear, toothed segments, and 5-15 cm long.

FLOWER HEADS. Showy and produced on long stalks; each flower head consists of outer ray flowers and inner disk flowers; the base is enclosed by bracts of two kinds, the inner ones pale yellow and pointed upward, the outer ones greenish and spreading. Blooms late August through October.

FRUITS. Yellowish black, hairy-margined, seedlike achenes 5-7 mm long, that have 2, 3, or 4 barbed bristles each.

DISTRIBUTION. Wet ground, fields, meadows, pastures, and roadsides throughout the state.

SIMILAR SPECIES. Spanishneedles, *Bidens bipinnata* L., a summer annual, has leaves that are 2-3 times pinnately divided and produce flowers that usually appear without ray florets. It blooms in August through October and grows in habitats similar to those of bearded beggarticks.

The genus *Bidens* includes the tickseeds, bur-marigolds, beggarticks, and spanishneedles. The common name refers to the 2 to 4 barbed awns on the seeds, which stick to the clothes of passersby and in that way may travel far from the parent plant.

Bearded Beggarticks
Bidens aristosa

Dandelion
Taraxacum officinale Weber

Composite Family
Asteraceae

EARMARKS. Plant has milky juice and a thick taproot; leaves basal; flower heads bright yellow.

ORIGIN. Eurasia, and possibly northern North America.

LIFE CYCLE. Perennial herb.

STEMS. Smooth, very short, and underground.

LEAVES. Five to 40 cm long; they vary in shape from oblong to spatulate and deeply toothed to slightly lobed, with the largest lobe at the tip; they narrow at the base into winged stalks.

FLOWER HEADS. Solitary, 2-5 cm wide, emerging from the tips of the hollow stems; the many tightly packed ray flowers are notched at the tips; the bracts at the base of the flower head are of two kinds, one pointing up and the other curving down. Blooms mostly March through May but is capable of blooming throughout the year.

FRUITS. Yellowish brown, seedlike achenes, each of which is 2-4 mm long and ribbed, terminating in a beak that is tipped with white hairs.

DISTRIBUTION. Roadsides, turf, pastures, gardens, waste places, and fallow and cultivated fields throughout the state.

The name *dandelion* comes from the French *dent de lion,* "lion's tooth," and refers to the deeply cut leaves with their toothlike margins. Early herbalists regarded the weed as one of the best greens for building up the blood and curing anemia.

Coffee made from dandelions is prepared from autumn roots cleaned, dried, and roasted until dark brown, then ground for use. The ground roots may be mixed with coffee or used alone. Dandelion beer is common in many parts of Canada; it is a rustic, fermented drink that is cheaper and less intoxicating than commercial beer.

Dandelion greens can also be purchased in cans in some specialty stores.

Dandelion
Taraxacum officinale

Orange Flowers

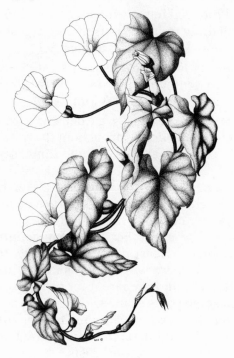

Velvetleaf
Abutilon theophrasti Medic.

Mallow Family
Malvaceae

EARMARKS. Leaves alternate, heart-shaped, velvety; flowers orangish yellow, solitary or in small clusters; fruits reminiscent of a crown.

ORIGIN. India.

LIFE CYCLE. Summer annual.

STEMS. Covered with short-branched or star-shaped hairs and up to 1.5 m tall.

LEAVES. Large, palmately veined, and 10-15 cm long, and have entire or toothed margins.

FLOWERS. Produced in the leaf axils; each is 15-25 mm wide with 5 partially united sepals, 5 petals, 5 stamens, and 1 pistil. Blooms July through September.

FRUITS. Rings of 10-17 hairy segments with outward-curving beaks; each segment contains several dark, flattened, kidney-shaped seeds about 3 mm long.

DISTRIBUTION. Waste places, gardens, vacant lots, and fallow and cultivated fields throughout the state. Velvetleaf is especially common on alluvial and sandy soils.

Velvetleaf was originally introduced into North America in the eighteenth century as a fiber crop. The colonists used it to make cordage, twine, and thread. Velvetleaf was imported from Russia and several other European countries and had become common in at least two states by 1829. Its popularity dwindled because there was no efficient way to remove the fiber from the stem and prepare it for use. It is still used as a fiber plant in some parts of the Old World.

The common names *pie-maker* and *butter-print* refer to the larger brown seed containers, which were used to stamp decorative patterns on butter or pie crusts.

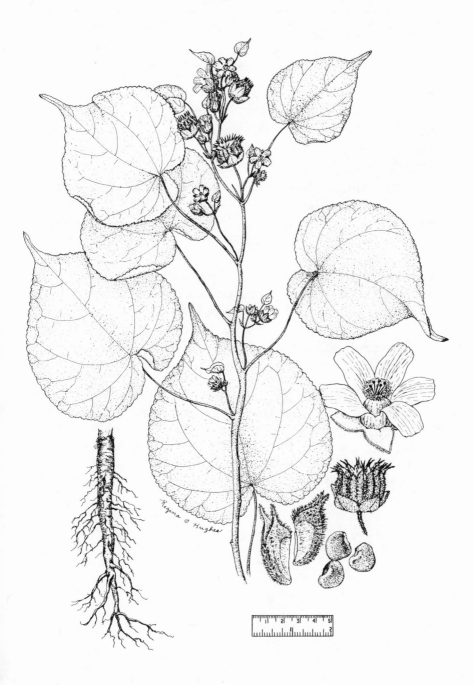

Velvetleaf
Abutilon theophrasti

Trumpetcreeper
Campsis radicans (L.) Seem.

Bignonia Family
Bignoniaceae

EARMARKS. Plant a woody vine; leaves opposite, pinnate; flowers showy, orangish red, trumpet-shaped.

ORIGIN. United States.

LIFE CYCLE. Perennial woody vine.

STEMS. Smooth, viney, and 6-12 m long.

LEAVES. Pinnate, having 5-11 sharp-pointed, toothed, ovate leaflets 4-8 cm long.

FLOWERS. In terminal clusters; they are large, 5-8 cm long and tubular with 5 spreading lobes. Blooms July through September.

FRUITS. Cigar-shaped capsules 10-22 cm long, with two longitudinal ridges, splitting open along two seams; the seeds, flattened and winged, are about 15 mm long.

DISTRIBUTION. Waste places, woodland borders, pastures, fencerows, and fallow and cultivated fields throughout the state. Often on trees, telephone polls, and barns.

This plant is also called *cow-itch*. People drinking milk from cows feeding on the vine may develop itchy skin. It is also said that when cows eat the plant an inflammation occurs on the udders and that those milking the cows develop rashes.

Other names that aptly describe the trailing habit of this weed are *devil's shoelaces* and *hell vine*.

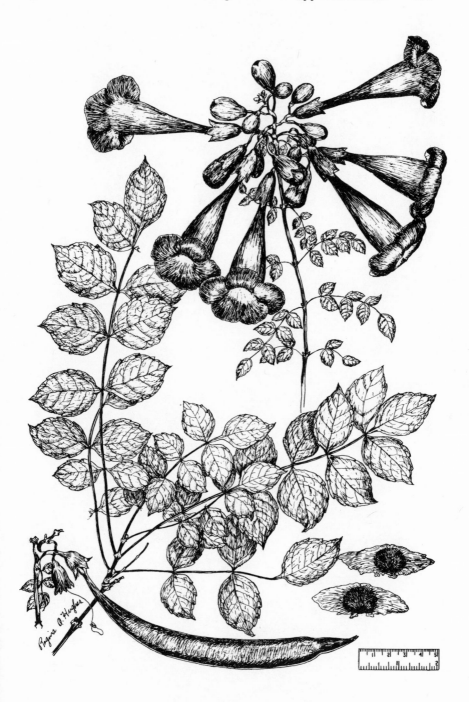

Trumpetcreeper
Campsis radicans

Pink Flowers

Common Mallow   Mallow Family
Malva neglecta Wallr.   Malvaceae

EARMARKS. Plant sprawling; leaves round to heart-shaped, long-stalked; flowers pale pink to lilac.

ORIGIN. Europe.

LIFE CYCLE. Winter annual.

STEMS. Prostrate, with tips that are usually turned up and slightly hairy; they often cover large areas and can grow to 3 dm long.

LEAVES. Alternate and toothed to shallowly lobed; they are hairy on both surfaces and 2-6 cm wide.

FLOWERS. Small and single or in clusters of 2-3 in the leaf axils; the petals are twice as long as the 5 sepals; 3 narrow leaflike bracts are under each flower. Blooms April through September.

FRUITS. Circles of 10-20 hairy segments, each segment with one dark reddish brown, kidney-shaped seed 1.3-8 mm long.

DISTRIBUTION. Roadsides, waste places, turf, gardens, pastures, barnyards, and fallow and cultivated fields throughout the state.

Although common mallow is considered a weed, it has both food and medicinal value. The Greeks, Romans, and Egyptians ate the seed pods, or "cheeses," in the morning in the belief that they would protect them from contracting any disease during the day.

An infusion of young leaves is said to cure colds and coughs.

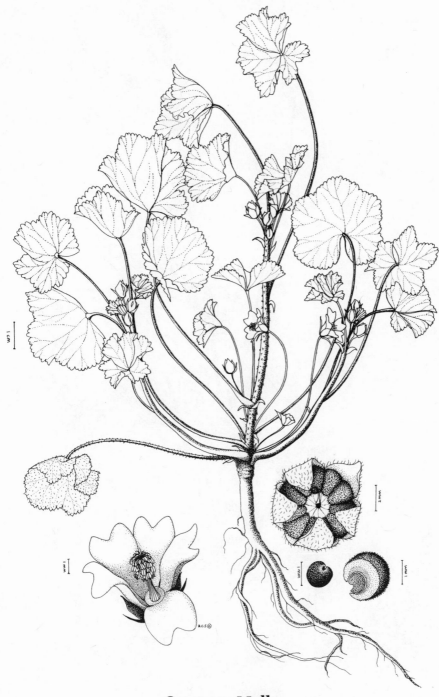

Common Mallow
Malva neglecta

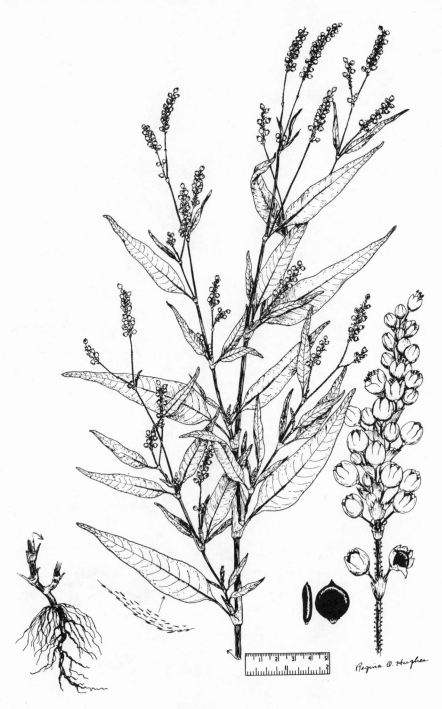

Pennsylvania Smartweed
Polygonum pensylvanicum

Pennsylvania Smartweed
Polygonum pensylvanicum L.

Knotweed Family
Polygonaceae

EARMARKS. Plant has jointed stems; leaves alternate, entire; flowers pink or purplish, occasionally white, in clusters.

ORIGIN. United States.

LIFE CYCLE. Summer annual.

STEMS. Branching, ascending to erect, green or reddish, smooth to slightly hairy, and up to 2 m high; the nodes are swollen.

LEAVES. Lanceolate to oval and 5-15 cm long; leaf stalks grow from a papery, hairless, cylindrical sheath (ocrea).

FLOWERS. Small and in dense, slightly nodding, cylindrical terminal clusters 1-6 cm long. Blooms June through September.

FRUITS. Black, broadly oval, flattish, glossy, seedlike achenes 2.2-3.5 mm long.

DISTRIBUTION. Roadside ditches, moist meadows, fields, gardens, waste places, streambanks, shores, and fallow and cultivated fields throughout the state.

SIMILAR SPECIES. Ladysthumb, *Polygonum persicaria* L., is a summer annual. It has hairs on the margins of the sheaths and narrow leaves, each of which often has a purple blotch on the blade. The pink, purple, or white flowers are in dense, cylindrical clusters. The fruits are black, broadly oval, flat, glossy, seedlike achenes about 1 mm long.

Some of the species in this large genus are sharp or peppery in taste, and their juices make mucous membrances of the eyes, nose, and mouth smart—hence the name *smartweed*.

Soaking the plant in vinegar and wrapping it around one's head is an old remedy believed to cure headache.

The smartweeds were taken to England from America around the eighteenth century, and were first grown as an ornamental by the Duchess of Bedford.

Wild Garlic
Allium vineale

Wild Garlic
Allium vineale L.

Lily Family
Liliaceae

EARMARKS. Plants bulbous or growing from bulbs; odor of garlic or onion; leaves alternate, hollow; flowers pinkish purple, in umbels, or sometimes replaced by small bulbs.

ORIGIN. Eurasia.

LIFE CYCLE. Perennial herb.

STEMS. Slender and leafy, the lower halves covered with sheathing leaf bases, which become stiff; they grow to 10 dm tall.

LEAVES. Two-ranked, smooth, bluish green, and cylindrical; they taper from the base to the tip.

FLOWERS. In umbels of either flowers and bulbs or only bulbs; the flowers when present have 6 perianth segments, 6 stamens, and 1 pistil each. Blooms May through July.

SEEDS. Dull black, 2-8 mm long, convex on the one side, and minutely bumpy.

DISTRIBUTION. Turf, waste places, and fields either fallow or cultivated with small grains or hay throughout Kentucky. Most common in the western part of the state in counties bordering the Ohio and Mississippi rivers.

Wild garlic has become one of the most noxious weeds to be introduced into the middle Atlantic and southeastern United States. Early records show that it was a serious problem in this country more than a century ago. Milk from livestock that have grazed on it has a garliclike flavor, which decreases its salability.

The genus *Allium* includes such important cultivated members as onion, garlic, shallot, chive, scallion, and leek.

Bouncingbet
Saponaria officinalis L.

Pink Family
Caryophyllaceae

EARMARKS. Leaves opposite, entire; flowers soft pink or white, with 5 separate petals, each indented at the tip.

ORIGIN. Europe.

LIFE CYCLE. Perennial herb.

STEMS. Smooth, usually branched, stout, and up to 8 dm tall.

LEAVES. Simple, stalkless, ovate or lanceolate, 3- to 5-veined, and 5-8 cm long.

FLOWERS. In dense terminal and axillary clusters; each has 5 sepals fused into a long tube with unequal teeth, 5 petals, 10 stamens, and 1 pistil with 2 styles; sometimes the flowers have more than the usual 5 petals and are referred to as *double*. Blooms June through September.

FRUITS. Capsules with four teeth that open to expose the numerous black, kidney-shaped seeds 1.8 mm long.

DISTRIBUTION. Roadsides, railroad embankments, pastures, open thickets, fencerows, waste places, and grain fields throughout the state.

Saponaria is derived from the Latin *sapo*, which means "soap" and refers to the lather produced in water by the crushed leaves. The leaves have a high saponin content as well as resin, gum, and mucilage, a combination that makes an excellent cleanser. Today, the soap from this plant is used in museums and historical houses to restore color and sheen to old fabrics, tapestries, brocades, and embroideries. It is also used to clean wools and other delicate fabrics such as silk. In Syria, Saudi Arabia, and a few other Middle Eastern countries, this plant is cultivated for soap-making.

Bouncingbet
Saponaria officinalis

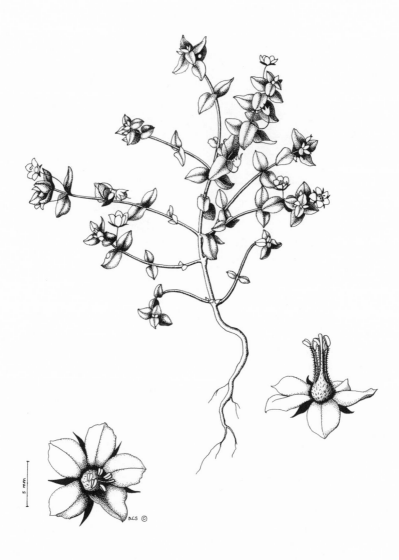

Scarlet Pimpernel
Anagallis arvensis

Scarlet Pimpernel
Anagallis arvensis L.

Primrose Family
Primulaceae

EARMARKS. Leaves opposite or in whorls of 3, entire; flowers scarlet to salmon-colored or occasionally pink, blue, or white, one in each leaf axil.

ORIGIN. Europe and the Mediterranean region.

LIFE CYCLE. Summer annual.

STEMS. Smooth, squarish, either erect or branched at the base, horizontally spreading, and up to 5 dm tall.

LEAVES. Stalkless, oval, smooth, glandular, dotted below, and up to 2 cm long.

FLOWERS. About 1 cm wide and produced on long, slender stalks; each has 5 sepals, 5 petals, and 5 stamens with bearded filaments. Blooms June through August.

FRUITS. Capsules containing many small, brown, 3-angled, pitted seeds 1.3 mm long.

DISTRIBUTION. Roadsides, turf, waste places, and fallow and cultivated fields throughout the state.

The generic name *Anagallis* is derived from the Greek *anagelao*, meaning "to laugh." It was believed that a tincture of this herb helped to overcome depression and melancholia.

Herbalists in the past considered this weed a surgical plant. They believed it had the power to draw out arrows, splinters, thorns, and other such objects embedded in the flesh.

This delicate plant is also known as *poor man's weatherglass* or as *shepherd's barometer* because the plant closes its flowers before or during rain.

Henbit
Lamium amplexicaule

Henbit

Lamium amplexicaule L.

Mint Family

Lamiaceae

EARMARKS. Stems square; leaves opposite, circular in outline; flowers pink with purple spots.

ORIGIN. Europe.

LIFE CYCLE. Winter annual.

STEMS. Smooth, 4-angled, and often decumbent and rooting at the lower nodes; they grow to 4 dm tall.

LEAVES. Variable; the upper ones are stalkless, clasping, circular to triangular, 1-2 cm long, palmately veined, and bluntly toothed; the lower ones are similar but produced on long stalks.

FLOWERS. Grouped in clusters of 6-10 in the upper leaf stalks; the corolla is 2-lipped, 1-1.5 cm long, and hairy on top. Blooms March through April and in the fall.

FRUITS. Brown nutlets mottled with white, blunt-tipped at the top, and 2-2.4 mm long.

DISTRIBUTION. Roadsides, gardens, turf, pastures, meadows, waste places, and fallow and cultivated fields throughout the state.

SIMILAR SPECIES. Red deadnettle, *Lamium purpureum* L., a winter annual, has opposite, short-stalked upper leaves that are heart-shaped and scalloped along the margins; the lower leaves are similar but are on long stalks. Blooms March through April and sometimes in the fall.

The generic name is derived from the Greek *lamos*, which means "throat" and refers to the wide-open throat of the corolla.

Joe-Pye Weed
Eupatorium fistulosum Barratt

Composite Family
Asteraceae

EARMARKS. Leaves in whorls of 4-7; flower heads pink or lilac, in fuzzy clusters.

ORIGIN. United States.

LIFE CYCLE. Perennial herb.

STEMS. Erect, purplish, hollow, covered with a whitish coating, and up to 2.5 m tall.

LEAVES. Rough, stalked, and narrowly elliptic; each leaf has one main vein and rounded, bluntly lobed teeth.

FLOWER HEADS. In rounded or dome-shaped clusters; individual flowers tubular and 4-6 mm long; the base of each flower head is enclosed by several greenish to brownish or purplish bracts. Blooms August through October.

FRUITS. Five-angled, seedlike achenes, slightly hairy on the ridges, and 3-4.5 mm long.

DISTRIBUTION. Moist, sunny areas along roads, and in waste places, fencerows, pastures, and meadows throughout the state.

Eupatorium is derived from the name of the king of Pontus, Mithridates Eupator, who was skilled in botany and physics. The common name, *joe-pye*, commemorates a New England herb doctor who is said to have cured typhus fever with a tonic made from the roots of one of the species.

Joe-Pye Weed
Eupatorium fistulosum

Blue Flowers

Alternate Leaves   170

Spotted Knapweed

Composite Family

Centaurea maculosa Lam.

Asteraceae

EARMARKS. Leaves alternate, deeply divided; flower heads thistlelike, blue, purplish pink, or white; bracts showy, black-tipped.

ORIGIN. Europe.

LIFE CYCLE. Biennial.

STEMS. Wiry, branched, slightly hairy, and 3-10 dm tall.

LEAVES. Variable, with the lower ones pinnately divided into narrow segments and the reduced upper, entire ones usually produced singly on the stem.

FLOWER HEADS. Numerous, arising from the tips of the branches and in the leaf axils; individual flowers are 1-2 cm wide and tubular, with the marginal ones enlarged. Blooms June through August.

FRUITS. Dark brown, seedlike achenes, each of which is softly hairy and has light-colored bristles at the top.

DISTRIBUTION. Dry, gravelly soils along roads and railroads, and in waste places, thickets, fencerows, pastures, and cultivated fields throughout the north and central regions of the state.

This species was introduced into this country as a contaminant of alfalfa seed. It is especially troublesome on rangelands in the northwestern United States.

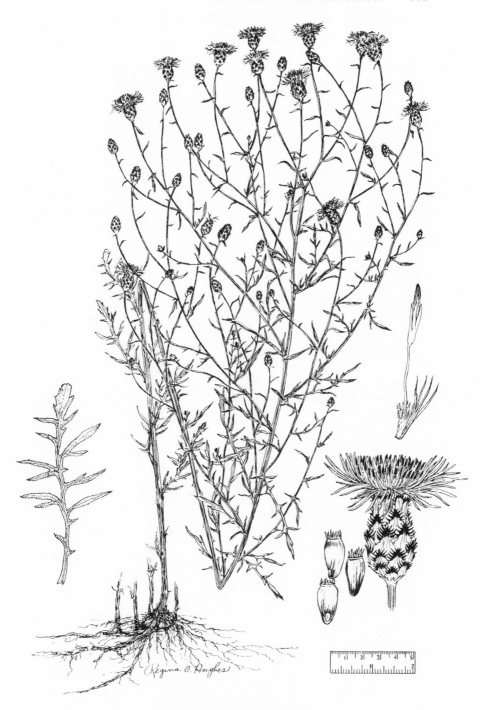

Spotted Knapweed
Centaurea maculosa

Chicory
Cichorium intybus

Chicory
Cichorium intybus L.

Composite Family
Asteraceae

EARMARKS. Leaves entire, lobed, or toothed; flower heads sky blue, pink, or occasionally white, dandelionlike, with notched tips.

ORIGIN. Mediterranean region.

LIFE CYCLE. Perennial herb.

STEMS. Erect, branched, hollow, and 5-20 dm tall; with age they become woody and reddish.

LEAVES. Alternate; the upper leaves are clasping, oblong to lanceolate, and 3-7 cm long; the larger basal and lower leaves are deeply or shallowly lobed, toothed, and clustered at the plant base, forming a rosette.

FLOWER HEADS. In small clusters or solitary on short branches; they are 2-3 cm wide; the base of each flower head is enclosed by several greenish bracts. Blooms June through October.

FRUITS. Light brown, mottled, obovate, 4- to 5-angled, seedlike achenes 2-3 mm long.

DISTRIBUTION. Roadsides, fencerows, fields, pastures, gardens, and fallow and cultivated fields throughout the state. Chicory is especially common in the Bluegrass Region, where it thrives on limestone soils.

Chicory was first introduced into the United States in 1785 by Governor Bowdoin of Massachusetts, who considered it a valuable salad green. It has since spread throughout the eastern, central, and western United States.

Chicory will ooze a white milk when scratched. Because of its similarity in appearance to human milk, in the mid-seventeenth century the British herbalist Nicholas Culpeper recommended chicory milk for nursing women pained by an abundance of milk. He also prescribed chicory for "sore eyes that are inflamed" because the beautiful blue flowers, like eyes, close at night "to sleep."

Chicory is used as a coffee additive, imparting to coffee a distinctive flavor and color. Before there were strict food laws, two million pounds of chicory were imported each year from Europe and used by coffee merchants, who claimed that it gave coffee a superior flavor.

Asiatic Dayflower

Dayflower Family

Commelina communis L.

Commelinaceae

EARMARKS. Leaves alternate, entire; flowers with two large blue petals.

ORIGIN. Asia.

LIFE CYCLE. Summer annual.

STEMS. Weak and slender; they root at the swollen nodes and grow to 8 dm long.

LEAVES. Lanceolate, simple, entire, parallel-veined, and 2-5 cm long; the leaf stalks sheath at the base.

FLOWERS. In clusters and open one at a time; each has 3 sepals and 3 petals; 2 of the petals are blue and broad, and the other is smaller and white; 6 yellow, and unequal stamens; the bract is green and heart-shaped. Blooms June through September.

FRUITS. Capsules contain a few greyish brown seeds, each 3-4 mm long, flat on one side, rounded on the other, and pitted on the surface.

DISTRIBUTION. Roadsides, railroads, gardens, barnyards, fields, waste places, and fallow and cultivated fields throughout the state.

The genus was named by Linnaeus, the great Swedish botanist, for three Dutch brothers named Commelin. Two of the brothers, represented by the upper petals, were well-known botanists, and the third brother, the insignificant lower petal, did nothing for science.

In the southwestern United States, the Navajo Indians prepared a drink from this plant and gave it to aged men and women to increase their potency. The tribes believed so strongly in the efficacy of the infusion that they gave it also to their stud animals.

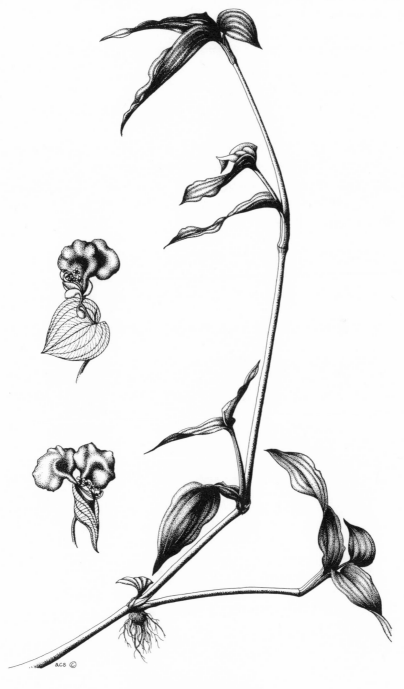

Asiatic Dayflower
Commelina communis

Spurred Anoda
Anoda cristata (L.) Schlecht.

Mallow Family
Malvaceae

EARMARKS.   Leaves alternate; flowers blue-violet, single in the leaf axils; fruits dark, crownlike.

ORIGIN.   Southwestern United States and Central and South America.

LIFE CYCLE.   Summer annual.

STEMS.   Hairy, freely branched, and up to 1 m tall.

LEAVES.   Ovate to triangular to 3-lobed, 5-10 cm long, coarsely toothed, and long-stalked.

FLOWERS.   One to 2 cm wide and produced on long slender stalks. Blooms July through October.

FRUITS.   Disks made up of 10-20 beaked segments; each segment contains one black kidney-shaped seed.

DISTRIBUTION.   Riverbanks, roadsides, and cultivated fields in a few counties. In the past three years, spurred anoda has spread from western Kentucky to the northeastern and far northern part of the state. If it continues to spread, it could become a troublesome weed in Kentucky.

Spurred anoda was first observed in cultivated fields in New Mexico and Arizona in the 1950s. It has spread rapidly and is now a troublesome weed in cotton and soybean fields in the midsouth region of the United States.

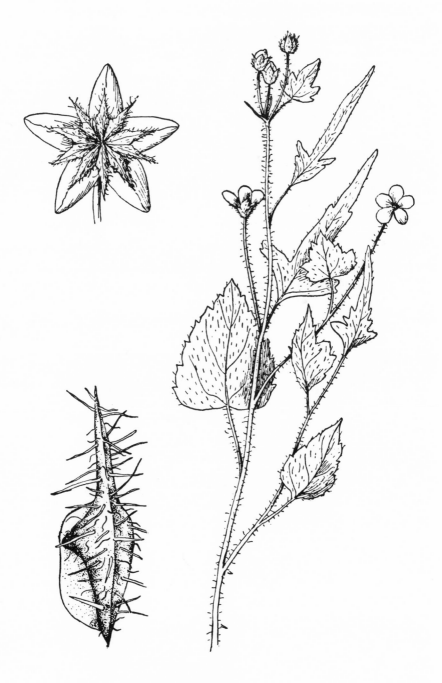

Spurred Anoda
Anoda cristata

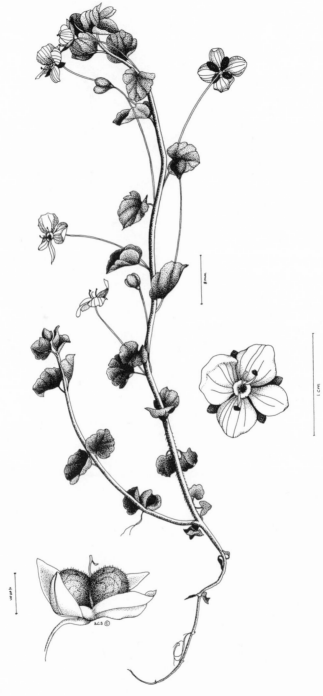

Birdseye Speedwell
Veronica persica

Birdseye Speedwell
Veronica persica Poir.

Figwort Family
Scrophulariaceae

EARMARKS. Plant low-growing; leaves alternate above, opposite below, toothed; flowers pale blue, with deeper blue lines.

ORIGIN. Eurasia.

LIFE CYCLE. Summer annual.

STEMS. Prostrate or ascending, often rooting at the lower nodes, branched, hairy, and 1-3 dm long.

LEAVES. Simple, round to ovate, short-stalked to clasping, and 0.5-2.5 cm long.

FLOWERS. Small, solitary, and produced on long, slightly recurved stalks that arise from the leaf axils; each has 4 sepals, 4 petals, and 2 stamens. Blooms March through May and sporadically during warm winter months.

FRUITS. Heart-shaped capsules 6-9 mm wide surrounded by 4 persistent sepals.

DISTRIBUTION. Gardens, turf, waste places, open gravelly fields, vacant lots, roadsides, and fallow and cultivated fields throughout the state.

SIMILAR SPECIES. Corn speedwell, *Veronica arvensis* L., is a low growing summer annual. The opposite, ovate leaves are palmately veined and have 2-4 blunt teeth on each side. The flowers are borne singly in the leaf axils and make up about two-thirds of the plant. The heart-shaped fruit capsules are 3-4 mm wide.

The genus name means "true image" and was named for St. Veronica. An early Christian legend depicts St. Veronica accompanying Christ on the trip to Calvary. Wiping his face with her handkerchief, she noticed a miraculous true image of his features in the cloth.

Purple Flowers

Common Burdock
Arctium minus

Common Burdock

Arctium minus Bernh.

Composite Family

Asteraceae

EARMARKS. Leaves alternate, oval, pale green beneath; flower heads purplish pink, burlike.

ORIGIN. Europe.

LIFE CYCLE. Monocarpic perennial.

STEMS. Erect, branched, stout, ridged, and up to 1.5 m tall.

LEAVES. Stalked, oval to elliptic, entire to wavy-margined, and up to 5 dm wide.

FLOWER HEADS. Short-stalked or stalkless, either solitary or in clusters of 2-3; the bases of the flower heads are enwrapped by overlapping bracts, each bract tipped with a hooked bristle. Blooms July through September.

FRUITS. Dark mottled, seedlike achenes 5-6 mm long.

DISTRIBUTION. Roadsides, vacant lots, waste places, barnyards, and fencerows throughout the state.

Common burdock was introduced into America by the early English and French colonists. In many parts of the world, this plant is believed to be a powerful antidote to evil spirits. For instance, the Iroquois Indians believed that witches used this plant to cause bad luck, accidents, and death by carving the root into the shape of the intended victim and stabbing the carving with a pointed object. One could counteract the witchcraft by drinking a tea made from the boiled roots.

In Albania, a similar superstition exists. If a person has been influenced by the demons of the forest, a priest must perform a ceremony to exorcise the evil spirits. Part of this ceremony consists of steeping bread in wine and spreading it on the leaves of common burdock.

In some countries, lads believed that they could catch bats by throwing burdock burs at them.

Musk Thistle
Carduus nutans L.

Composite Family
Asteraceae

EARMARKS. Flower heads large, solitary, purplish pink or sometimes white, often nodding; leaves alternate, spiny.

ORIGIN. Eurasia.

LIFE CYCLE. Biennial.

STEMS. Stout, erect, spiny, branched, and 3-10 dm tall.

LEAVES. Light green with spines extending down the stem, giving a winged appearance; each lobe is tipped with a light-colored spine.

FLOWER HEADS. Terminal on long naked stalks; the base of each flower head is enclosed by many greenish to purplish bracts, each bract tipped with a yellowish spine. Blooms June through September.

FRUITS. Smooth, yellowish brown, striated, seedlike achenes with tufts of silky hairs at the tips.

DISTRIBUTION. Roadsides, waste places, fencerows, pastures, and fallow and cultivated fields throughout the state.

Musk thistle, also known as *nodding thistle*, has spread rapidly in Kentucky and is listed as one of the ten most troublesome weeds in the state. It was first brought to the attention of the University of Kentucky's College of Agriculture in the 1940s, when it was found along the Warren–Logan County line. Since then, it has spread and grows in all of the 120 counties.

Raw, peeled stems of musk thistle have a taste similar to artichokes and are tender and flavorful when cooked.

Musk Thistle
Carduus nutans

Field Thistle
Cirsium discolor

Field Thistle
Cirsium discolor (Muhl.) Spreng.

Composite Family
Asteraceae

EARMARKS. Leaves deeply divided, white-woolly beneath; flower heads large, solitary, purplish pink to occasionally white.

ORIGIN. United States.

LIFE CYCLE. Biennial.

STEMS. Stout, woody, hollow, freely branched, and 1 to 3 mm tall.

LEAVES. Variable; the lower ones are green above, distinctly veined, and divided nearly to the middle; the lobes bear thin, bristly tips; the upper stem leaves are similar but progressively smaller; below each flower head are long, spine-tipped bracts.

FLOWER HEADS. Terminal and 3.5-4 cm high; the base of each flower head is enclosed by many long narrow bracts, each bract tipped with a prickle. Blooms August through October.

FRUITS. Light brown, glossy, seedlike achenes 4-5 mm long, each with a yellow beak and tufted silky white hairs at the tip.

DISTRIBUTION. Roadsides, fields, thickets, gardens, pastures, fencerows, and woodland borders throughout the state.

SIMILAR SPECIES. Canada thistle, *Cirsium arvense* (L.) Scop., is a perennial with deep rhizomes. It has many small, pink-purple flower heads. The oblong to lanceolate leaves are irregularly lobed with yellowish spines on the margins. Blooms June through October. Bull thistle, *Cirsium vulgare* (Savi) Tenore, a biennial, has prickly lobed wings on the stem. The leaves are pale or webbed beneath, pinnately divided with lance-shaped lobes each tipped with a straw-colored prickle. Blooms July through September.

The generic name comes from the Greek word meaning "swelling vein" and refers to the blood vessels thistles are claimed to heal.

Field thistle contains a substance that can curdle milk and aid in the cheese-making process. The flower heads are mashed to release a renninlike material. This liquid is very strong, and only a small amount is needed to curdle large quantities of milk.

Tall Ironweed

Composite Family

Vernonia gigantea (Walt.) Trel.   Asteraceae
[Syn. *Vernonia altissima* Nutt.]

EARMARKS. Leaves alternate, toothed; flower heads red-violet or purple, in clusters.

ORIGIN. United States.

LIFE CYCLE. Perennial herb.

STEMS. Stout, loosely branched at the top, and up to 2 m tall.

LEAVES. Loosely spreading, lanceolate to narrowly ovate, 4-8 cm wide, sharply toothed, and rough on the surface below.

FLOWER HEADS. Many, in a much-branched cluster that blooms from the center outward; the base of each flower head is enclosed by overlapping purplish bracts. Blooms late July through October.

FRUITS. Ribbed, seedlike achenes, each crowned with a tuft of tawny brown hairs.

DISTRIBUTION. Waste places, damp meadows, pastures, vacant lots, barnyards, roadsides, railroad embankments, and fallow and cultivated fields throughout the state.

The generic name honors the seventeenth-century English botanist William Vernon.

Tall Ironweed
Vernonia gigantea

Tall Morningglory

Ipomoea purpurea (L.) Roth

Morningglory Family

Convolvulaceae

EARMARKS. Plant is a vine; leaves alternate, heart-shaped; flowers purple, blue, or white; sepals hairy at the base.

ORIGIN. Tropical America.

LIFE CYCLE. Summer annual.

STEMS. Trailing or twining, hairy to smooth, and up to 5 m long.

LEAVES. Heart-shaped, entire or rarely 3-lobed, and abruptly pointed at the tip.

FLOWERS. In clusters of 1-7 on long axillary stalks; each has 5 sepals and 5 petals that form a flaring tube 4-7 cm long. Blooms June through September.

FRUITS. Capsules have 4-6 brownish black seeds 3.5-4.5 mm long, each with 1 rounded surface and 2 flat surfaces.

DISTRIBUTION. Roadsides, railroad embankments, gardens, turf, waste places, fencerows, pastures, and fallow and cultivated fields throughout the state.

It is believed that Cortés, the Spanish explorer, collected tall morningglory seeds from the Aztecs in Mexico and was the first to send them back to monastery gardens in Spain.

The entire plant can be used to prepare a laxative.

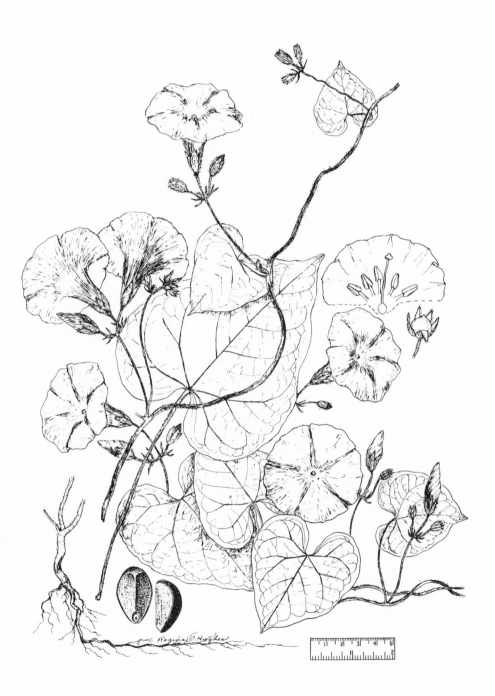

Tall Morningglory
Ipomoea purpurea

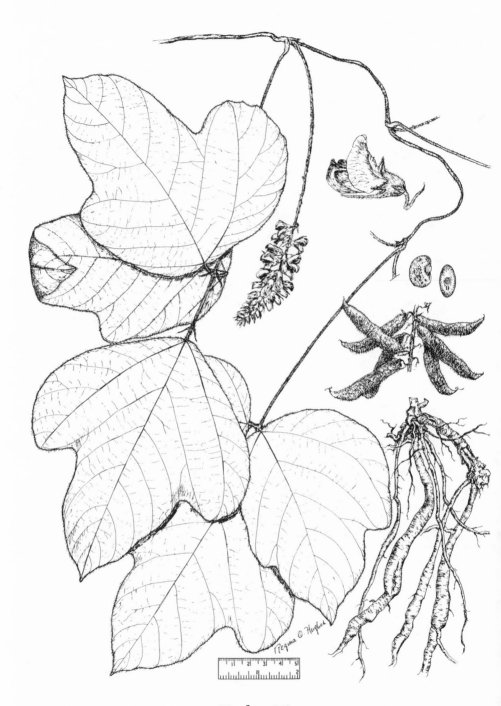

Kudzu-Vine
Pueraria lobata

Kudzu-Vine
Pueraria lobata (Willd.) Ohwi

Legume Family
Fabaceae

EARMARKS. Plant is a vine; leaves alternate, with 3 leaflets; flowers deep purple, pealike.

ORIGIN. Eastern Asia.

LIFE CYCLE. Perennial vine.

STEMS. High-climbing, twining, herbaceous to woody, hairy when young, and up to 30 m long.

LEAVES. Produced on long, hairy stalks; they have 3 broadly ovate leaflets that are entire or 2- to 3-lobed.

FLOWERS. Have a fragrance similar to Concord grapes; they are in dense clusters on long stalks in the leaf axils, and each has 5 sepals and 5 petals; the upper petal has a distinct yellowish green spot in the center. Blooms August through September.

FRUITS. Brown, fuzzy pods 4-5 cm long that contain nearly round seeds.

DISTRIBUTION. Usually grows on trees and telephone poles on roadsides, railroad embankments, vacant lots, woodland borders, and fields throughout the southeastern part of the state, where severe infestations occur. Kudzu-vine is also found in the central, southern, northern, and western counties.

In 1876, the Japanese exhibited this Asian plant at the Philadelphia Centennial Exposition. Americans who saw this unknown ornamental vine became enthusiastic about using it in their landscapes. It was grown later in the southern United States for livestock, fodder, and pasturage. In 1935, the Soil Conservation Service began using it as a soil binder on farmland that had suffered severe soil erosion. The plant soon became known as *king kudzu*. By 1955, however, it had become a curse, spreading over trees, shrubs, gardens, fences, and anything else that stood in its path. Because it grows 100 feet a season, it has become one of the most aggressive, troublesome weeds in the southeastern United States.

Johnsongrass
Sorghum halepense (L.) Pers.

Grass Family
Poaceae

EARMARKS. Grass has rhizomes; leaf has a prominent midvein; inflorescence open, much-branched.

ORIGIN. Mediterranean region.

LIFE CYCLE. Perennial herb.

STEMS. Stout, erect, and up to 2 m tall.

LEAF BLADES. Simple, smooth, 1-2 cm wide; each has a prominent midvein.

SHEATHS. Smooth and green to purplish.

LIGULES. Whitish, finely toothed, and about 4 mm long.

AURICLES. Absent.

SPIKELETS. In pairs along the branches of the inflorescence (one of each pair stalkless), oval, purplish to straw-colored, sometimes with protruding bristles. Blooms June through September.

FRUITS. Reddish brown, oval grains 2.5 mm long.

DISTRIBUTION. Pastures, waste places, thickets, vacant lots, moist meadows, roadsides, and railroad embankments throughout the state.

SIMILAR SPECIES. Shattercane, *Sorghum bicolor* (L.) Moench., a summer annual, is a variable forage sorghum that has escaped and become a troublesome weed in crops throughout Kentucky. The stems grow to 2 m tall and the leaves resemble other sorghums. The large flower clusters often droop to one side, and the seeds, which mature in August and October, are surrounded by dark brown to reddish, shiny scales.

The botanical name means "sorghum from Halepa," the area of Syria in which the grass supposedly originated.

It is often used for hay or pasturage and can be dangerously poisonous under certain conditions. When they freeze, the leaves develop a poison fatal to grazing cattle. Cut hay and silage should be cured for six weeks before being used.

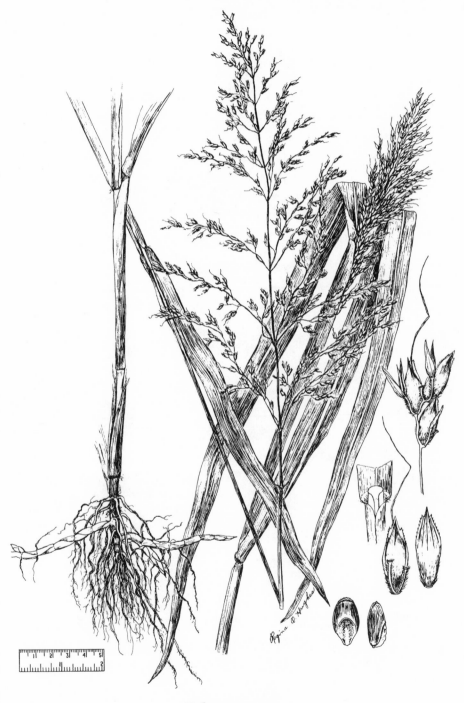

Johnsongrass
Sorghum halepense

Horsenettle
Solanum carolinense

Horsenettle

Nightshade Family

Solanum carolinense L.

Solanaceae

EARMARKS. Plant has stout, straw-colored prickles; leaves alternate; flowers pale violet and star-shaped.

ORIGIN. United States.

LIFE CYCLE. Perennial herb.

STEMS. Erect, loosely branched, prickly, and 2-6 dm tall.

LEAVES. Simple, oblong to ovate, and 7-12 cm long; they are coarsely toothed to lobed and have straw-colored prickles on the midrib and leaf stalk.

FLOWERS. In clusters on prickly stalks at the branch tips; each has 5 sepals, 5 united petals, and 5 fused yellowish orange stamens that surround 1 pistil. Blooms May through September.

FRUITS. Smooth, round, orange berries 1-2 cm wide that have juicy pulp with many yellowish, somewhat circular, glossy seeds about 2 mm long.

DISTRIBUTION. Roadsides, gardens, waste places, pastures, barnyards, and fallow and cultivated fields throughout the state. Horsenettle is especially common in sandy, gravelly soil.

Because of the prickly nature of the plant, horsenettle can reduce the quality of grazing pastures. It can also be a serious problem in fields in which no-till production is practiced.

Bitter Nightshade
Solanum dulcamara L.

Nightshade Family
Solanaceae

EARMARKS. Plant twining; leaves alternate, usually lobed; flowers purple, rarely white, star-shaped; ripe berries red.

ORIGIN. Europe.

LIFE CYCLE. Perennial herbaceous vine.

STEMS. Slender, twining, woody at the base, and up to 3 m long.

LEAVES. Have two lobes at the base and are entire-margined.

FLOWERS. In small, open clusters; each has 5 persistent sepals, 5 narrow petals, and 5 yellow stamens surrounding 1 pistil. Blooms May through October.

FRUITS. Pulpy, bright red berries that contain many dull, light yellow, thin, somewhat circular seeds about 2-2.5 mm wide.

DISTRIBUTION. Roadsides, gardens, barnyards, vacant lots, thickets, pastures, fencerows, and cultivated fields throughout the state.

Livestock and poultry have been poisoned by eating the foliage, stems, and berries, which contain a deadly glucoside, *solanine.*

The generic name *Solanum* comes from the Latin *solamen,* which means "comfort, solace" and refers to the plant's soothing narcotic properties.

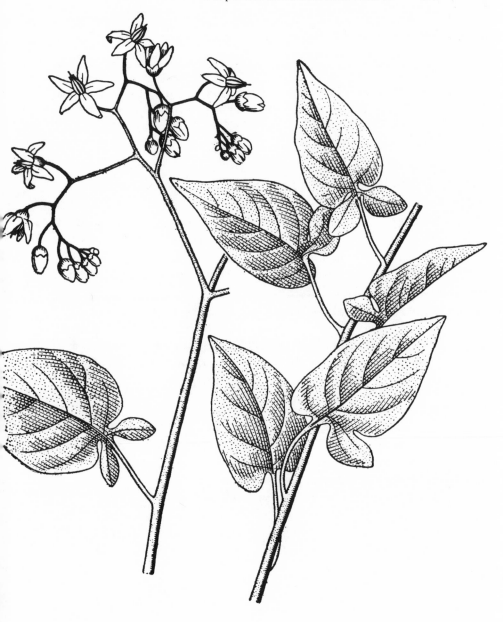

Bitter Nightshade
Solanum dulcamara

Common Milkweed   Milkweed Family
Asclepias syriaca L.   Asclepidaceae

EARMARKS.   Plant has milky sap; leaves opposite or whorled, distinctly veined; flowers purplish pink to green, in clusters; seed pods warty.

ORIGIN.   United States.

LIFE CYCLE.   Perennial herb.

STEMS.   Unbranched, stout, erect, covered with short, downy hairs, and 5-15 dm tall.

LEAVES.   Oblong to elliptic, 1.2-7 cm long, entire-margined, pale green above and whitish beneath.

FLOWERS.   Fragrant, bell-shaped, long-stalked, and in clusters hanging from the tips of the branches and in the leaf axils. Blooms July through September.

FRUITS.   Pods, 1-3 cm long, produced on recurved stalks and containing flat, brownish, ovate to obovate, winged seeds that are tipped with tufts of long silky hairs.

DISTRIBUTION.   Roadsides, woodland borders, thickets, waste places, fencerows, and fallow and cultivated fields throughout the state.

The genus was named by Linnaeus in honor of Homer's physician, Asclepios, who became the guardian god of medicine.

Common milkweed has had a few medicinal uses throughout history. For instance, the roots were ground up and used as a supposed treatment of syphilis, and the juice was said to make warts disappear.

The silky hair from the fruit pods was used to make beds and pillows far better than those made with feathers or cotton.

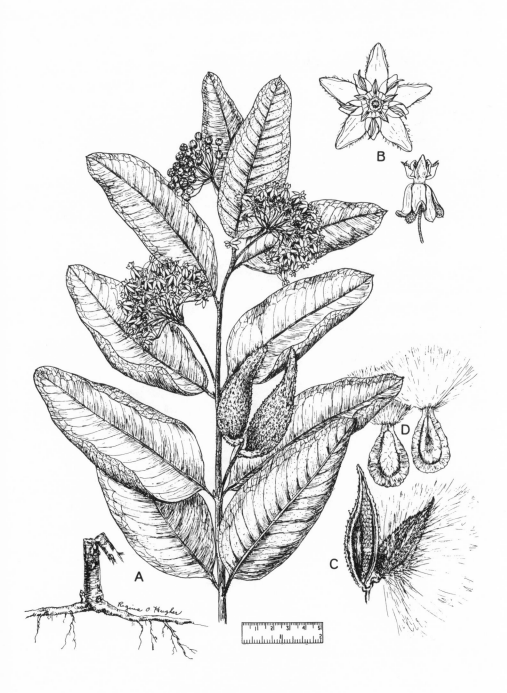

Common Milkweed

Asclepias syriaca

Mistflower

Eupatorium coelestinum L.

Composite Family

Asteraceae

EARMARKS. Leaves opposite, distinctly 3-veined; flower heads purplish blue to occasionally white, in broad, flat-topped clusters.

ORIGIN. United States.

LIFE CYCLE. Perennial herb.

STEMS. Reddish with a few long hairs, and up to 1 m tall.

LEAVES. In pairs; they are triangular to ovate, bluntly to sharply toothed, and stalked.

FLOWER HEADS. Made up of as many as 40 individual disk flowers; the base of each flower head is enclosed by several greenish, long-pointed bracts. Blooms August through September.

FRUITS. Greyish brown, pitted, 5-ribbed, seedlike achenes that are tapered at the bottom and 3 mm long.

DISTRIBUTION. Moist meadows, thickets, woodland borders, streambanks, pastures, and roadsides throughout the state.

This attractive plant, sometimes called *perennial ageratum*, does well in perennial flower beds. It spreads easily because of the creeping underground stems.

Mistflower
Eupatorium coelestinum

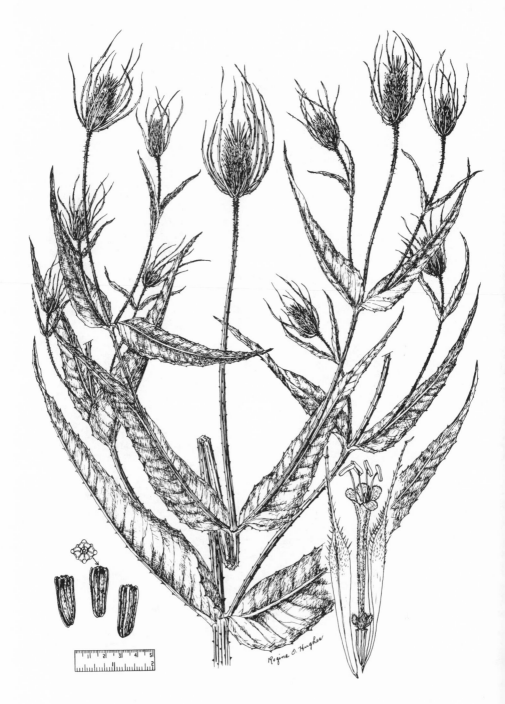

Teasel
Dipsacus fullonum

Teasel

Dipsacus fullonum L.
[Syn. *Dipsacus sylvestris* Huds.]

Teasel Family
Dipsacaceae

EARMARKS.   Stems with downward pointing prickles; leaves opposite, prickly on the midvein below; flowers pale purple to white, in terminal, thistlelike heads; fruiting pods brown, cylindrical, prickly.

ORIGIN.   Europe.

LIFE CYCLE.   Monocarpic perennial.

STEMS.   Erect, stout, prickly on the ridges, and up to 12 dm tall.

LEAVES.   In a basal rosette the first year; they are oblanceolate with wavy margins; the upper, narrow leaves clasp the stem.

FLOWERS.   Produced in dense, egg-shaped clusters at the tips of the stems; the leaves below the flowers are prickly and long-tapering. Blooms July through September.

DISTRIBUTION.   Roadsides, railroad embankments, pastures, old fields, waste places, and woodland borders throughout the state. Teasel is especially common on limestone soils in the Bluegrass Region.

The roots of teasel are boiled in wine and pounded into a smooth cream used as a folk remedy for ulcers and warts. The water collected in the hollow formed by the paired and joined leaves is said to soothe inflammation of the eyes and to keep the face fair.

Gypsies used the dried teasel heads as combs, hence the name *gypsy comb*.

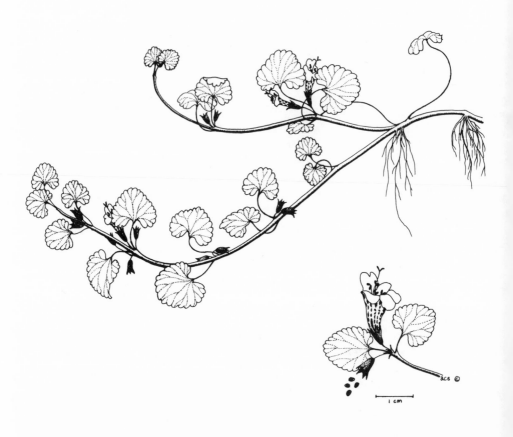

Ground Ivy
Glechoma hederacea

Ground Ivy
Glechoma hederacea L.

Mint Family
Lamiaceae

EARMARKS. Plant creeping; leaves opposite, stalked, rounded; flowers purplish pink to blue, tubular.

ORIGIN. Eurasia.

LIFE CYCLE. Perennial herb.

STEMS. Four-angled, smooth, and creeping; they root at the nodes and grow to 7 dm long.

LEAVES. Palmately veined, orbicular to kidney-shaped, bluntly toothed, and 1.3 cm wide.

FLOWERS. Produced in axillary clusters; the corolla is 2-lipped with an arched upper lip and 3-lobed lower lip; there are 4 stamens. Blooms April through June.

FRUITS. Dark brown nutlets in groups of 4 (or fewer by abortion) and 1.5-2 mm long.

DISTRIBUTION. Roadsides, gardens, turf, woods, waste places, and rich shaded areas by dwellings and fields throughout the state.

Ground ivy, also called *alehoof*, has been associated with the ale industry for hundreds of years. It was the most widely used seasoning in brewing ale until the German discovery of the value of hops. Ground ivy was believed to flavor and preserve the ale as well as to help it clear.

Another name for this weed is *gill-over-the-ground*. The word *gill* is from a French word that means "fermented ale."

This aromatic herb contains a bitter, volatile oil that is poisonous to cattle that eat the green or dried leaves mixed in hay or fodder.

Mint Perilla

Mint Family

Perilla frutescens (L.) Britt.

Lamiaceae

EARMARKS. Plant rank smelling; leaves opposite, green to purplish bronze; flowers purple or white, small.

ORIGIN. Eastern Asia.

LIFE CYCLE. Summer annual.

STEMS. Purplish, square, and up to 1 m tall.

LEAVES. Long-stalked and oblong to broadly ovate; they are coarsely toothed, pointed, and 8-15 cm long.

FLOWERS. In loose, elongated clusters produced at the top of the stem or in the upper leaf axils; they are small, each with a 2-lipped calyx and 5 rounded petals of which the lowest one is the largest. Blooms August through September.

FRUITS. Four rounded, net-veined nutlets enclosed by the enlarged, papery calyx.

DISTRIBUTION. Roadsides, waste places, barnyards, and pastures, especially in shady, moist areas throughout the state.

A variety of this species is often cultivated for its attractive bronze and purple foliage. The leaves are also used in certain Oriental dishes and can be purchased in cans.

The seeds are a source of oil used in the manufacture of printer's ink, artificial leather, paper umbrellas, and waterproofing for clothing.

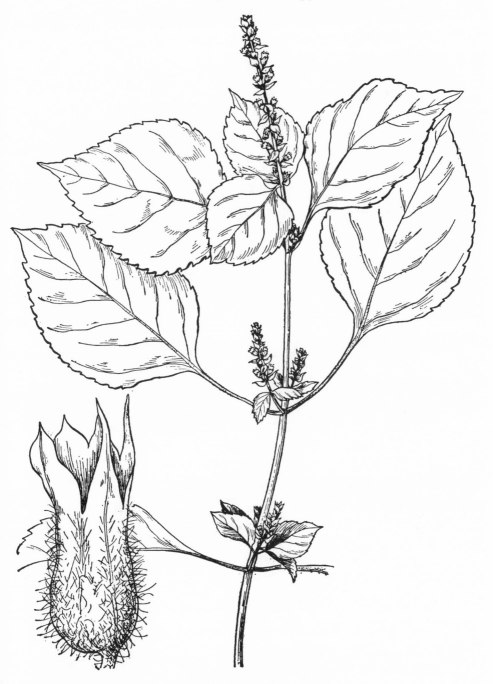

Mint Perilla
Perilla frutescens

Green Flowers

Alternate Leaves 212

Smooth Pigweed
Amaranthus hybridus

Smooth Pigweed
Amaranthus hybridus L.

Amaranth Family
Amaranthaceae

EARMARKS. Leaves alternate, oval; flower parts indistinguishable, greenish yellow, in bristly fingerlike clusters.

ORIGIN. Eastern United States and Central and South America.

LIFE CYCLE. Summer annual.

STEMS. Ridged and often reddish at the base and up to 2 m tall.

LEAVES. Long-stalked, ovate to rhombic-ovate, darker green above, distinctly veined below, and 4-13 cm long.

FLOWERS. Either all male or all female and small, with 1-3 stiff bracts that are equal to, or up to twice as long as, the 5 sharp-pointed sepals; the bracts and sepals surround either 1 pistil or 5 stamens. Blooms July through October.

FRUITS. Utricles, each containing one dark, circular, reddish brown to black, shiny seed 1 mm wide.

DISTRIBUTION. Roadsides, waste places, pastures, and fallow and cultivated fields throughout the state.

SIMILAR SPECIES. Redroot pigweed, *Amaranthus retroflexus* L., a summer annual, has green bracts on the female flowers that are 2-3 times as long as the round-tipped sepals. This species is infrequent to rare in Kentucky.

Several species closely related to smooth pigweed were grown as a major food crop of the Aztecs in Mexico. Even today, the amaranths are grown in parts of Mexico as well as by the Indians of the southwestern United States.

Some archeologists suggest that the Ozark-Bluff dwellers, who lived in northern Arkansas and southern Missouri, may have cultivated smooth pigweed, as the seeds have been found in archeological remains.

The plant is also a symbol of immortality because long after it is gathered the dry red, bristly bracts retain their freshness.

Spiny Amaranthus
Amaranthus spinosus

Spiny Amaranthus
Amaranthus spinosus L.

Amaranth Family
Amaranthaceae

EARMARKS. Leaves alternate, with a pair of spines at the base of the leaf stalk; flowers greenish yellow, bristly.

ORIGIN. Tropical America.

LIFE CYCLE. Summer annual.

STEMS. Reddish, stout, upright, and branched; they grow to 1 m tall.

LEAVES. Long-stalked, with rhombic-ovate to lanceolate blades, dull green, distinctly veined below, and 3-6 cm long.

FLOWERS. In clusters; the female flowers are in dense, axillary clusters and the male flowers are in terminal clusters; the bracts are shorter than the 5 yellowish green sepals. Blooms July through September.

FRUITS. Utricles, each containing one small, dark brown, circular seed about 1 mm wide.

DISTRIBUTION. Roadsides, waste places, barnyards, and fallow and cultivated fields throughout the state. Spiny amaranth is a problem especially in pastures and on thin soils, where infestations may be severe.

SIMILAR SPECIES. Tumble pigweed, *Amaranthus albus* L., a summer annual, has stems that are whitish green and spineless. Common throughout the state.

Many species in this genus are noxious weeds and only a few are cultivated. In some parts of the United States, young, tender plants of spiny amaranth are cooked and eaten as a vegetable. In tropical America, a decoction made from the plant is used for bathing and is said to reduce fevers. It is also applied to external inflammations.

Common Ragweed
Ambrosia artemisiifolia L.

Composite Family
Asteraceae

EARMARKS. Leaves deeply divided; flower heads greenish yellow, mostly in terminal clusters.

ORIGIN. United States.

LIFE CYCLE. Summer annual.

STEMS. Smooth to long-hairy, simple or branched, and up to 15 dm tall.

LEAVES. Stalked, usually alternate on the upper part of the plant and opposite below, 5-10 cm long, and cut into many bluntly toothed or lobed segments.

FLOWER HEADS. Of two kinds: the tiny female heads are in the leaf axils and the showier male heads are in small, inverted clusters at the top of the plant. Blooms August through October.

FRUITS. Seedlike achenes enclosed in a light brown, woody case that is longitudinally ribbed and ends in 5-10 short, spiny projections.

DISTRIBUTION. Roadsides, vacant lots, pastures, waste places, woodcuts, and fallow and cultivated fields throughout the state.

SIMILAR SPECIES. Giant ragweed, *Ambrosia trifida* L., a summer annual, has leaves that are unlobed to deeply 3- to 5-lobed. It is found throughout the state, especially in moist ground along the floodplains of the Ohio and Mississippi rivers. Blooms August through September.

The pollen of the ragweeds is an enemy of hay fever sufferers. Long before allergenic preparations were available, ragweed was used as an astringent said to open closed nasal passages and to relieve constant sneezing.

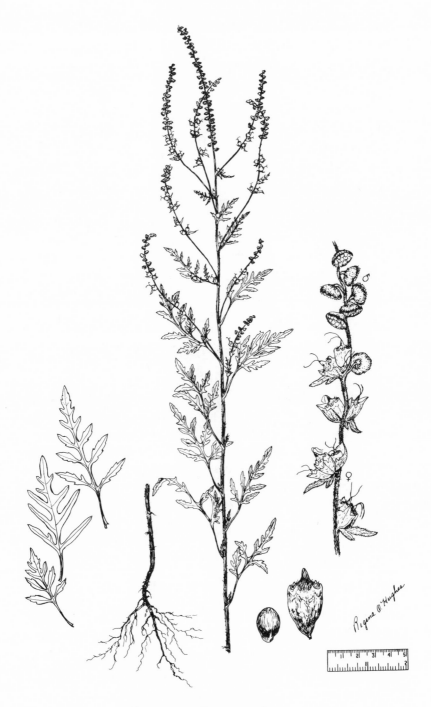

Common Ragweed
Ambrosia artemisiifolia

Annual Marshelder
Iva annua

Annual Marshelder

Iva annua L.
[Syn. *Iva ciliata* Willd.]

Composite Family
Asteraceae

EARMARKS.   Leaves opposite below, alternate above; flower heads in clusters, greenish white.

ORIGIN.   United States.

LIFE CYCLE.   Summer annual.

STEMS.   Stout, rough, hairy, and up to 20 dm tall.

LEAVES.   Pale green on slender stalks; each is broadly lanceolate to ovate, downy beneath, coarsely toothed, pointed, and 5-15 mm long.

FLOWER HEADS.   Small and nodding, in dense clusters in the leaf axils; the heads are nearly enclosed by greenish bracts. Blooms July through September.

FRUITS.   Black, pear-shaped, ribbed, seedlike achenes 2.5 mm long and 1.5 mm wide.

DISTRIBUTION.   Roadsides, riverbanks, waste places, and moist open fields throughout the western half of the state and scattered eastward. Annual marshelder is especially troublesome in pastures.

The large achenes of this plant were a food source for early man. Remains of them have been found in rock shelters left by the bluff dwellers of the Ozarks and Kentucky.

Common Cocklebur
Xanthium strumarium L.

Composite Family
Asteraceae

EARMARKS.   Plant coarse; leaves alternate, often 3-lobed and 3-veined; flower parts indistinguishable, green, in the leaf axils; bur light brown.

ORIGIN.   Eurasia, Central America, and eastern United States.

LIFE CYCLE.   Summer annual.

STEMS.   Erect, bushy, grooved, red-spotted, roughly hairy, and 2-8 dm tall.

LEAVES.   Stalked, with the petioles about as long as the blades, they are broadly ovate to heart-shaped, roughly hairy, and coarsely toothed.

FLOWER HEADS.   Produced in separate parts of the plant; the small male flowers are in short, terminal spikes which drop after the pollen has been shed; the female flowers are in axillary clusters. Blooms August through September.

BURS.   Hard, oval to oblong, and with hooked prickles; each contains two female flowers.

FRUITS.   Two dark brown, oblong, seedlike achenes that are flat, each with a pointed apex, and 1-1.5 cm long; they are enclosed in the burs.

DISTRIBUTION.   Roadsides, riverbanks, pastures, waste places, moist meadows, fencerows, and fallow and culti-vated fields throughout the state.

The generic name is derived from the Greek *xanthos*, meaning "yellow" and referring to the plant's thick yellow sap. In Greece, the sap was used as a hair dye.

Swine, sheep, and cattle often eat this poisonous plant. The hooks on the fruits can cause injury by matting the fruits, or burs, together into balls in the stomachs and intestines of animals, often causing death. The burs also get entangled in the fur of grazing animals and can be an annoyance to the owners.

Common Cocklebur
Xanthium strumarium

Common Lambsquarters
Chenopodium album

Common Lambsquarters
Chenopodium album L.

Goosefoot Family
Chenopodiaceae

EARMARKS. Leaves alternate, whitish grey beneath; flower parts indistinguishable, greenish or purplish.

ORIGIN. Eurasia.

LIFE CYCLE. Summer annual.

STEMS. Erect, conspicuously tan-and-red-ridged, branched above, and up to 20 dm tall.

LEAVES. Variable; the lower leaves are broadly ovate to rhombic and wavy margined or broadly toothed; the upper ones are narrow, clasping, and covered with a white mealy substance on the lower side, especially when young.

FLOWERS. Borne in dense, rounded clusters at the tips of the branches and in the leaf axils; they are small with 5 sepals and no petals. Blooms July through October.

FRUITS. Utricles, each containing one shiny, black or reddish brown, lens-shaped seed 1-1.5 mm wide.

DISTRIBUTION. Roadsides, waste places, barnyards, pastures, fallow and cultivated fields throughout the state.

SIMILAR SPECIES. Mexicantea, *Chenopodium ambrosioides* L., a summer annual, has yellow, resinous glands on the oblong to lanceolate leaves and is very aromatic. The flowers are similar to common lambsquarters and bloom July through September.

Common lambsquarters is considered one of the world's most troublesome weeds. It is a prolific seed producer, as one average-sized plant can produce over 70,000 seeds. The common name is thought to be a corruption of "lammas quarter," an ancient festival in Britain.

This plant has been used since prehistoric times. In Alberta, Canada, a Blackfoot archeological site was found with a storage room containing 4-5 liters of cleaned *Chenopodium album* seeds. Today, the tender young plants are collected by the Indians and others of the southwestern United States, who boil and eat them like spinach. The seeds are ground into a flour resembling that of buckwheat.

In 1750 Peter Kalm, a student of Linnaeus's, reported that settlers in what are now New Jersey and Pennsylvania gave their children mexicantea seeds to help them expel worms.

Burcucumber
Sicyos angulatus L.

Gourd Family
Cucurbitaceae

EARMARKS. Plant is a vine that climbs by tendrils; leaves alternate, large, 3- to 5-lobed; flowers bell-shaped, greenish white.

ORIGIN. United States.

LIFE CYCLE. Summer annual.

STEMS. Longitudinally ridged, hairy, and up to 15 m long; they climb or cling with 3-forked tendrils.

LEAVES. Rough, 10-20 cm wide, heart-shaped in general outline, and with 3-5 lobes that are either blunt or sharp-pointed and palmately veined.

FLOWERS. Unisexual, with the male (long-stalked) and the female (short-stalked) on separate stalks from the leaf axils; they have 5 petals that are fused below. Blooms late June through September.

FRUITS. Broad, prickly, ovate, 12 mm long; each contains one light brown seed with two whitish knobs at the base.

DISTRIBUTION. Roadsides, railroad embankments, woodland borders, waste places, gardens, cultivated fields, and along watercourses throughout the state, but especially common in riverbottoms in western Kentucky.

Some persons are sensitive to handling the prickly fruits of this species and will break out in a rash from such contact.

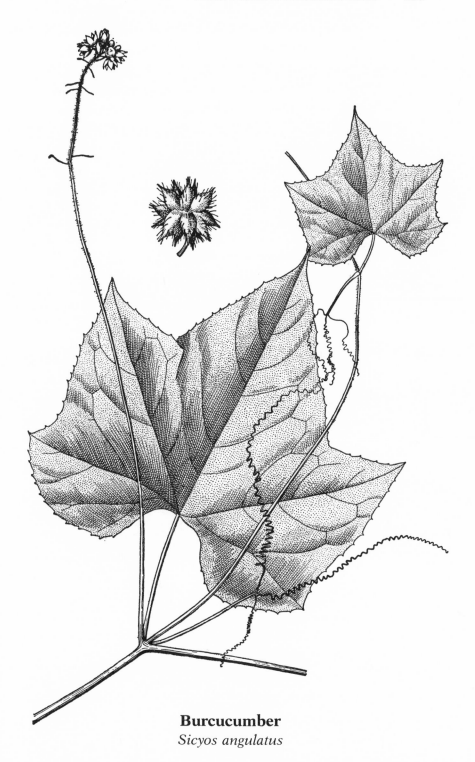

Burcucumber
Sicyos angulatus

Broadleaf Signalgrass

Grass Family

Brachiaria platyphylla (Griseb.) Nash.   Poaceae

EARMARKS. Plant is a grass; inflorescence made up of fingerlike clusters along the upper part of the stem.

ORIGIN. Southeastern and southcentral United States.

LIFE CYCLE. Summer annual.

STEMS. Green to purplish-tinged, smooth, and 3-6 dm tall.

LEAF BLADES. Short and wide, widest near or at the base; the sheath margins are densely hairy.

LIGULES. A ring of dense hairs.

AURICLES. Absent.

SPIKELETS. Oval, pointed, and in a row along one side of each branch of the cluster. Blooms throughout the summer.

FRUITS. Grains 4-5 mm long, enclosed in greenish yellow, transversely ridged spikelet scales.

DISTRIBUTION. Scattered in pastures, gardens, and cultivated fields throughout the western half of the state.

This southern grass has just recently spread into croplands in Kentucky and is becoming a troublesome weed throughout its range.

The generic name is derived from the Latin *brachium*, "arm," and refers to the armlike clusters along the upper part of the stem.

Broadleaf Signalgrass
Brachiaria platyphylla

Large Crabgrass
Digitaria sanguinalis

Large Crabgrass
Digitaria sanguinalis (L.) Scop.

Grass Family
Poaceae

EARMARKS. Plant is a grass with a purplish tinge through-out; inflorescence made up of 2-10 long, fingerlike clusters at the top of the stem.

ORIGIN. Europe.

LIFE CYCLE. Summer annual.

STEMS. Erect or spreading, smooth, often rooting at the nodes, and 2-10 dm tall.

LEAF BLADES. Green or purplish and 5-12 cm long, with a prominent midvein and silky hairs on both surfaces.

SHEATHS. Greenish red with long hairs.

LIGULES. White, membranous, and 1-2 mm long.

AURICLES. Absent.

SPIKELETS. Oval, pointed, and closely arranged in two rows on one side of a curved branch of the cluster. Blooms June through September.

FRUITS. Light yellow, oval grains that are finely granular and 1.5-2 mm long.

DISTRIBUTION. Gardens, turf, pastures, waste places, and fallow and cultivated fields throughout the state.

SIMILAR SPECIES. Smooth crabgrass, *Digitaria ischaemum* (Schreb.) Muhl., a summer annual, has smooth stems, sheaths, and leaf blades. The inflorescence is made up of several thin, threadlike clusters not spreading from a single point. Common throughout Kentucky.

Large crabgrass is also known as *finger-grass* and *twitch-grass.* The generic name comes from *digitus*, meaning "finger."

Large crabgrass was introduced into the United States in 1849 by the U.S. Patent Office. It was brought from Europe to help alleviate the need for good forage due to the increasing number of imported domestic animals. By the late nineteenth century, farmers had abandoned the plant and replaced it with such profitable crops as corn and wheat. Since then, this species has spread throughout most of the United States and has become a most troublesome weed.

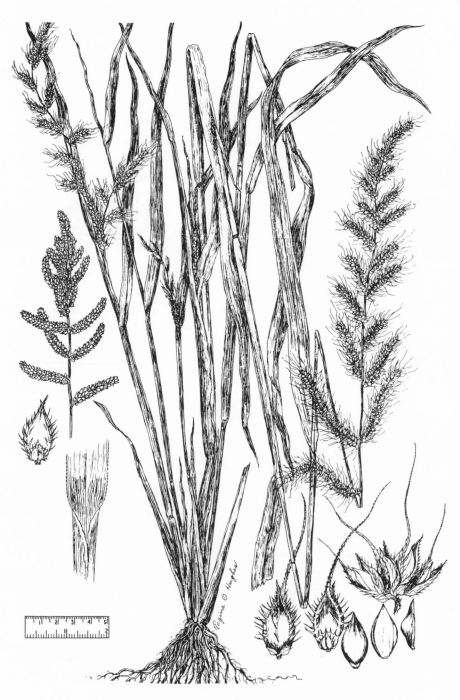

Barnyardgrass
Echinochloa crusgalli

Barnyardgrass
Grass Family
Echinochloa crusgalli (L.) Beauv.   Poaceae

EARMARKS. Plant is a grass; leaves have neither ligules nor auricles.

ORIGIN. Europe and Asia.

LIFE CYCLE. Summer annual.

STEMS. Bent at the base and up to 1.2 m tall.

LEAF BLADES. Smooth, narrow, often wavy-margined, and 1-2 dm long; they have prominent white midribs.

SHEATHS. Almost closed.

SPIKELETS. Oval, pale green to purplish, and densely arranged along one side of each branch of the cluster, sometimes with protruding, short to long bristles. Blooms June through September.

FRUITS. Tan grains, longitudinally ridged on the convex side, and 2.5-3.5 mm long.

DISTRIBUTION. Roadside ditches, mudflats around ponds, waste places, moist meadows, and fallow and cultivated fields throughout the state.

American Indians gathered the large seeds of barnyardgrass before they became too ripe. The seeds were ground between stones to make a flour, which was mixed with milk and water to prepare baked goods. The dried seeds were also used in soups and stews.

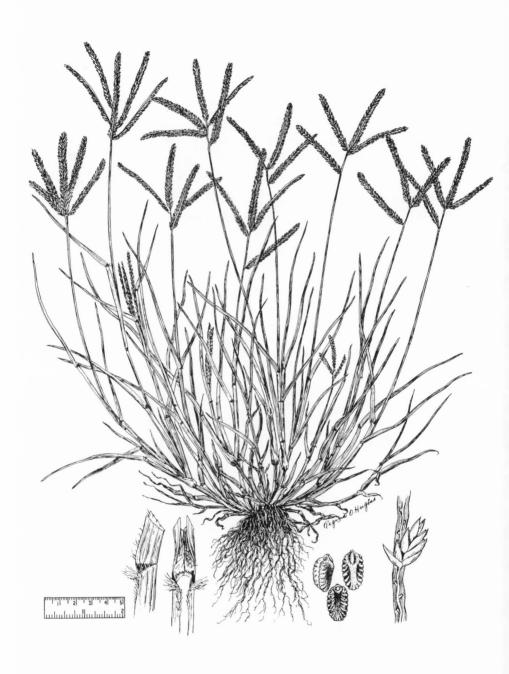

Goosegrass
Eleusine indica

Goosegrass
Eleusine indica (L.) Gaertn.

Grass Family

Poaceae

EARMARKS. Tufted grass; stems flattened and silvery white at the base; inflorescence in clusters arranged like the vanes of a windmill.

ORIGIN. Old World.

LIFE CYCLE. Summer annual.

STEMS. Branched, erect or prostrate, silvery white at the base, and up to 5 dm tall.

LEAF BLADES. Flat, pale green, and 3-9 mm wide.

SHEATHS. Overlapping and loose, with long hairs along the margin.

LIGULES. Short and toothed.

AURICLES. Absent.

SPIKELETS. Somewhat flattened and densely arranged in a row along one side of each branch of the cluster. Blooms June through September.

FRUITS. Reddish brown grains 1-1.5 mm long that are ridged and granular.

DISTRIBUTION. Turf, pastures, waste places, gardens, road-sides, and fallow and cultivated fields throughout the state.

The Arabs and various nomadic groups in Africa gathered the seeds and ground them into a flour used in bread and soups in times of famine.

Fall Panicum
Panicum dichotomiflorum Michx.

Grass Family
Poaceae

EARMARKS. Plant is a tufted grass; stem zig-zag; inflorescence open, much-branched.

ORIGIN. United States.

LIFE CYCLE. Summer annual.

STEMS. Ascending or spreading and up to 2 m tall; the lower nodes are enlarged and shiny.

LEAF BLADES. Rough, sometimes hairy, lanceolate, and 2-5 dm long, with a prominent white midrib.

SHEATHS. Rough and hairless.

LIGULES. Form a ring of white hairs 1-2 mm long.

AURICLES. Absent.

SPIKELETS. Oval, short-stalked, pointed, and light green. Blooms July through September.

FRUITS. Dull yellow grains 1.5 mm long.

DISTRIBUTION. Gardens, waste places, and fallow and cultivated fields throughout the state.

SIMILAR SPECIES. Witchgrass, *Panicum capillare* L., a summer annual, has stout and occasionally branched stems. The stems, sheaths, and leaf blades are densely hairy. It is not as troublesome in croplands as fall panicum.

This large genus has many species throughout the world. Several of them are cultivated for hay and forage.

Fall Panicum
Panicum dichotomiflorum

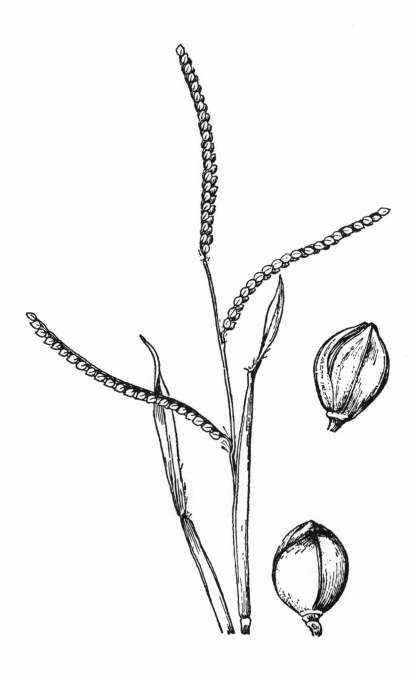

Field Paspalum
Paspalum laeve

Field Paspalum

Paspalum laeve Michx.

Grass Family

Poaceae

EARMARKS. Plant is a tufted grass; inflorescence in 2-8 fingerlike ascending clusters.

ORIGIN. United States.

LIFE CYCLE. Perennial herb.

STEMS. Slender and up to 1.2 m high; several grow from one base.

LEAF BLADES. Flat or folded, smooth to hairy, and 5-25 cm long.

SHEATHS. Covered with long hairs.

LIGULES. Long and membranous.

AURICLES. Absent.

SPIKELETS. Circular, short-stalked, and in a row on one side of each branch of the cluster. Blooms July through September.

FRUITS. Yellowish brown, ovate to orbicular, and 3 mm wide with the midvein terminating at a distinct point.

DISTRIBUTION. Roadsides, turf, gardens, waste places, thickets, meadows, pastures, and cultivated fields throughout the state.

This genus has many members distributed throughout the warmer regions of the world. A few are cultivated for forage and for soil erosion control.

Giant Foxtail

Setaria faberi Herrm.

Grass Family

Poaceae

EARMARKS. Plant is a grass with large, green, nodding, cylindrical flower clusters at the top of the stem.

ORIGIN. China.

LIFE CYCLE. Summer annual.

STEMS. Erect, or weak and falling over, and up to 2 m tall.

LEAF BLADES. Short hairs on the upper surface; the distinct midrib is white to pale green.

SHEATHS. Edged with fine hairs on some parts of the margin.

LIGULES. Form a ring of short, white hairs.

AURICLES. Absent.

SPIKELETS. Ovate and about 3 mm long; there are 3-6 bristles at the base of each spikelet. Blooms June through October.

FRUITS. Oval, greenish, transversely wrinkled grains.

DISTRIBUTION. Roadsides, railroad embankments, gardens, turf, waste places, pastures, fencerows, and fallow and cultivated fields throughout the state.

SIMILAR SPECIES. There are two other summer annual species of *Setaria* common throughout Kentucky in croplands and pastures. Yellow foxtail, *Setaria lutescens* (Weigel) Hubb. [Syn. *Setaria glauca* (L.) Beauv.] has a dense, cylindrical yellow cluster with each spikelet surrounded by 5 to 20 bristles. The leaf sheaths are smooth and the leaf blade is hairy only at the base. Green foxtail, *Setaria viridis* (L.) Beauv., has a dense, erect to nodding cluster that is green or purple as in var. *robusta purpurea* (robust purple foxtail). Each spikelet is surrounded by 1 to 3 bristles. The upper leaf surfaces are smooth.

There are several weedy species of foxtail in the United States. Giant foxtail, named for its discoverer, Ernest Faber, was introduced from China into the United States probably in contaminated Chinese millet seed. It was first reported in 1939 in northern Virginia, and since then has spread throughout most of the eastern United States. In Kentucky, it is one of the ten most troublesome weeds.

Giant Foxtail
Setaria faberi

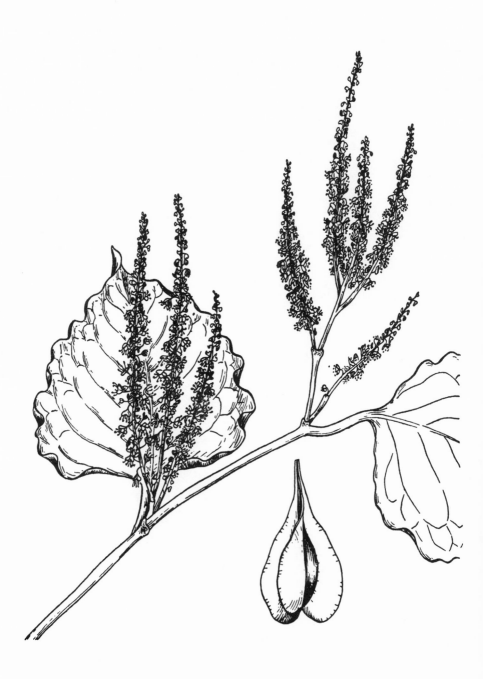

Japanese Knotweed
Polygonum cuspidatum

Japanese Knotweed

Knotweed Family

Polygonum cuspidatum Sieb. & Zucc. Polygonaceae

EARMARKS. Plant shrublike with jointed stems; leaves alternate, entire; flowers greenish white, in either erect or drooping clusters.

ORIGIN. Japan.

LIFE CYCLE. Perennial herb.

STEMS. Stout, mottled, smooth, often shrubby, and up to 3 m tall.

LEAVES. Broadly ovate, 8-15 cm long, and straight or slightly rounded at the base.

FLOWERS. Either all male or all female; they are produced in numerous clusters in the upper leaf axils; the male flowers are erect and the female flowers droop. Blooms August through October.

FRUITS. Triangular, shiny, seedlike achenes 3-4 mm long covered with widely winged sepals.

DISTRIBUTION. Roadsides, railroad embankments, riverbanks, waste places, gardens, vacant lots, woodland thickets, and pastures throughout the state.

The young shoots, collected in the spring, are steamed and served as a substitute for asparagus or rhubarb.

Curly Dock
Rumex crispus

Curly Dock

Buckwheat Family

Rumex crispus L.

Polygonaceae

EARMARKS. Stems with a papery cylindrical sheath at each joint; leaves with wavy margins; flowers greenish to reddish brown at maturity.

ORIGIN. Eurasia.

LIFE CYCLE. Perennial herb.

STEMS. Smooth and ridged; they have swollen joints and grow to 1 m tall.

LEAVES. Alternate and mostly basal; the basal leaves are bluish green, simple, narrow, and rounded to nearly heart-shaped at the base; the stem leaves are similar.

FLOWERS. In dense clusters; each has 6 sepals; the outer 3 sepals are small and inconspicuous and the inner, large sepals are heart-shaped and bear a plump grainlike structure at the base. Blooms July through September.

FRUITS. Glossy, reddish brown, triangular, seedlike achenes 1.5-2.5 mm long.

DISTRIBUTION. Turf, gardens, vacant lots, pastures, meadows, roadsides, and fallow and cultivated fields throughout the state.

SIMILAR SPECIES. Broadleaf dock, *Rumex obtusifolius* L., a perennial herb, has large broad lower leaves up to 15 cm wide with heart-shaped bases. Fruits are chocolate brown, lustrous, triangular, and 2.5 mm long. Red sorrel, *Rumex acetosella* L., a perennial herb, grows to 4 dm tall. The slender stems have alternate, arrow-shaped leaves. The fruits (developing only on the plants bearing female flowers) are dark reddish brown, blunt, and 1.5 mm long. Both species grow in habitats similar to those of curly dock and bloom from June through September.

The leaves of the red sorrel are pleasantly tart and refreshing. When eaten, they are said to produce a feeling of well-being.

Golden Brown Flowers

Quackgrass

Agropyron repens (L.) Beauv.

Grass Family

Poaceae

EARMARKS. Plant is a grass with extensive underground creeping rhizomes; inflorescence of terminal clusters that may be loosely or densely flowered.

ORIGIN. Europe.

LIFE CYCLE. Perennial herb.

STEMS. Tufted or mat-forming, light green, smooth and sometimes curved at the base; they grow to 12 dm tall.

LEAF BLADES. Greyish green to bluish, slightly hairy to smooth on both surfaces, and ribbed with a conspicuous midrib on the underside.

SHEATHS. Slightly hairy to smooth.

LIGULES. Short and finely toothed.

AURICLES. Small, greenish white, and clawlike, and clasp the stem.

SPIKELETS. Straw-colored, lance-shaped to oblong, and arranged in two rows, one row on each side of the cluster. Blooms June through September.

FRUITS. Yellowish brown grains 3.5-5 mm long.

DISTRIBUTION. Gardens, turf, waste places, pastures, and fallow and cultivated fields throughout the state.

Quackgrass, an aggressive weed, was introduced into New England before 1751. It spread westward during the early years, possibly in contaminated bromegrass seed, hay, and straw. It is a valuable hay and an excellent cover for soil erosion in steep gullies and embankments.

The ancient Egyptians made a flour from ground quackgrass roots and used it to extend their flour supply in times of shortage. Even today in parts of Italy, the roots are harvested and sold in outdoor markets for grinding into flour.

Dog-grass is another name commonly used for this weed. It is said that sickly dogs will eat it to cure their illnesses.

Quackgrass
Agropyron repens

Broomsedge

Andropogon virginicus

Broomsedge

Andropogon virginicus L.

Grass Family

Poaceae

EARMARKS. Plant is a tufted grass, turning orange-brown when dry; inflorescence of short clusters scattered among leaves along the stems, each cluster with conspicuous cottony hairs.

ORIGIN. United States.

LIFE CYCLE. Perennial herb.

STEMS. Smooth, slightly branched above, and up to 9 dm tall.

LEAF BLADES. Green to pale green, flat or folded, tapered, and 3-9 dm long.

SHEATHS. Strongly compressed and bearing a few long hairs.

LIGULES. White, collarlike, slightly toothed, and bear a few hairs.

AURICLES. Absent.

SPIKELET CLUSTERS. Exceeded by a reddish brown leaf; each spikelet is very narrow, straw-colored, and pointed, and has a protruding bristle. Blooms August through November.

FRUITS. Yellowish green, linear, glossy grains 1.5-2 mm long.

DISTRIBUTION. Pastures, dry meadows, waste places, and roadsides throughout the state.

Broomsedge, with its orange-brown color, is a common sight throughout Kentucky. Brooms used to be made from its straight branches. The generic name *Andropogon* means "bearded like an old man" and refers to the fluffy white covering of the seeds. The species was named by Linnaeus, who thought that the grass originated in Virginia and that it was more common in that state than anywhere else.

Japanese Brome
Bromus japonicus Thunb.

Grass Family
Poaceae

EARMARKS. Plant is a grass; leaves greyish green; inflorescence branched, open, drooping to one side.

ORIGIN. Eurasia.

LIFE CYCLE. Winter annual.

STEMS. Erect, stout, hairy at the base, and up to 1 m tall.

LEAF BLADES. Each is densely hairy, 2-4 mm wide, and has a prominent midrib below.

SHEATHS. Covered with short hairs.

LIGULES. White, torn, and about 2 mm long.

AURICLES. Absent.

SPIKELETS. Stalked, oval to lanceolate, and 7-9 mm long; each has several protruding bristles. Blooms June through August.

FRUITS. Straw-colored, narrow grains 7-8 mm long, with protruding bristles.

DISTRIBUTION. Roadsides, fencerows, meadows, waste places, and cultivated fields throughout the state.

SIMILAR SPECIES. Cheat, *Bromus secalinus* L., a winter annual, has leaf blades that are mostly hairless, usually twisted and with prominent midribs below. The ligules are brownish yellow and torn, and the sheaths are without hairs. The wavy bristles, 3-5 mm long, are often deciduous.

The genus contains many important forage and range grasses. Other species are serious pests because the barbed fruits can cause injury to grazing animals by getting into their eyes, nostrils, and mouths.

Japanese brome is a palatable grass that often grows in overgrazed rangelands and offers temporary pasture in early spring.

Japanese Brome

Bromus japonicus

Bermudagrass

Cynodon dactylon (L.) Pers.

Grass Family

Poaceae

EARMARKS. Plant is a stoloniferous grass, wiry, often mat-forming; inflorescence made up of 3-7 fingerlike clusters that radiate from the end of the stem.

ORIGIN. Tropical America.

LIFE CYCLE. Perennial herb.

STOLONS. Flat, creeping, with a dead bladeless sheath at each joint.

STEMS. Erect or ascending, wiry, flattened, and up to 3 dm high.

LEAF BLADES. Grey-green, 3 mm wide, and hairy or smooth except for a small tuft of hairs just above the collar.

SHEATHS. Smooth with a few hairs on the upper surface.

LIGULES. Form a ring of white hairs on the upper surface.

AURICLES. Absent.

SPIKELETS. Straw-colored to brown, flattened, pointed, and crowded on one side of each branch of the cluster. Blooms July through September.

FRUITS. Oval, reddish orange grains 1.5 mm long.

DISTRIBUTION. Roadsides, turf, gardens, pastures, waste places, and cultivated fields throughout the state.

Bermudagrass, which is planted in lawns, golf courses, and pastures, is considered one of the worst hay fever causing grasses in the United States. Exactly when it arrived in America is uncertain. James Meese, in his "Geological Account of the United States" (1807), stated, "Probably as important a grass as any in the southern states is bermudagrass, which grows with great luxuriance and propagates with astonishing rapidity by means of its numerous jointing, every one of which takes roots."

In Mexico, the entire plant is made into a decoction thought to heal complaints of the liver, spleen, and kidneys.

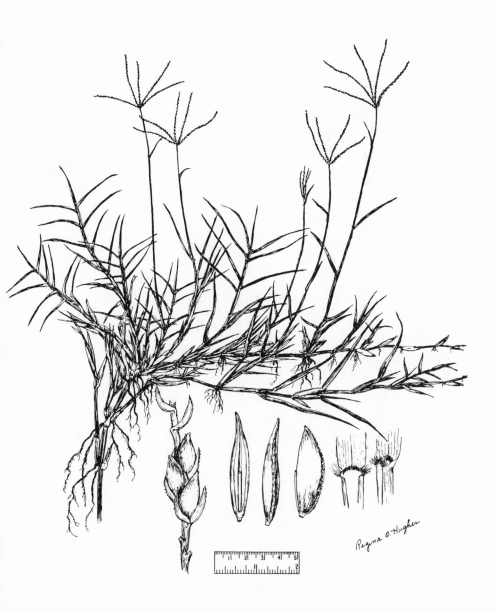

Bermudagrass
Cynodon dactylon

Yellow Nutsedge
Cyperus esculentus

Yellow Nutsedge
Cyperus esculentus L.

Sedge Family
Cyperaceae

EARMARKS. Plant has small underground tubers; stems yellowish green, grasslike; leaves mostly basal.

ORIGIN. United States and Eurasia.

LIFE CYCLE. Perennial herb.

STEMS. Simple, triangular, and up to 9 dm tall.

LEAVES. Three-ranked, narrow, and surrounded by a closed sheath about as long as the stem.

FLOWERS. In clusters of straw-colored to brown spikelets that are flattened and emerge at right angles to the stalk; the leaves under each cluster are much longer than the spikelets. Blooms July through September.

FRUITS. Yellowish brown, seedlike achenes that are granular-striate, 3-angled, linear to oblong, and 1.2-2 mm long.

DISTRIBUTION. Roadsides, gardens, turf, waste places, and fallow and cultivated fields throughout the state.

Yellow nutsedge, also called *northern nutgrass*, is a troublesome weed in the northeastern United States. It competes with crops and reduces quality and yield in potatoes, corn, tomatoes, beans, and peppers. It spreads easily and reproduces by rhizomes, tubers, and seeds.

In southern Europe, western Asia, and parts of Africa, it is grown for its edible tubers. These have a taste similar to almonds and may be cooked, ground into flour, or made into a cold drink. The species name means "edible," and aptly describes this plant.

Buckhorn Plantain
Plantago lanceolata L.

Plantain Family
Plantaginaceae

EARMARKS. Plant has narrow, basal leaves only; flowers golden brown, in short cylindrical clusters.

ORIGIN. Eurasia.

LIFE CYCLE. Perennial herb.

STEMS. Simple, leafless, slightly hairy, and 2-8 dm tall.

LEAVES. Narrow, stalked, and 5-30 cm long; each has 3-5 prominent veins.

FLOWERS. Arranged in dense clusters at the tips of the stems and are difficult to distinguish individually; each has 4 sepals, 4 translucent petals, 4 long stamens, and 1 pistil with a long style. Blooms late May through September.

FRUITS. Brown capsules 3-3.5 mm long, each containing 2 dark brown, glossy, elliptic seeds 1.5-2.5 mm long.

DISTRIBUTION. Roadsides, turf, waste places, gardens, meadows, and fallow and cultivated fields throughout the state.

SIMILAR SPECIES. Blackseed plantain, *Plantago rugelii* Dcne., a perennial herb, has broadly oval to elliptic basal leaves that are reddish at the base. The golden brown flowers are in dense, elongated, terminal clusters. Common throughout the state.

The Indians called the plantains *the white man's foot* because the plants accompanied the white man wherever he traveled in the New World.

The leaves were used by early American settlers as a medicine thought to cure snake and insect bites. The Indians heated the leaves and applied them as a wet dressing alleged to heal wounds.

Buckhorn Plantain
Plantago lanceolata

Gray Flowers

Alternate Leaves   260

Nimblewill
Muhlenbergia schreberi J.F. Gmel.

Grass Family
Poaceae

EARMARKS. Plant is a creeping grass; stems wiry, grayish blue; inflorescence made up of threadlike clusters.

ORIGIN. United States.

LIFE CYCLE. Perennial herb.

STEMS. Creeping or ascending, rooting at the lower nodes, and up to 6 cm long.

LEAF BLADES. Flat and loosely spreading.

SHEATHS. Loose and smooth.

LIGULES. Short, membranous, and torn, with tufts of hairs on either side.

AURICLES. Absent.

SPIKELETS. Grayish tan, 2 mm long, long-pointed, and densely arranged in a cluster, each spikelet with a delicate protruding bristle. Blooms August through October.

FRUITS. Reddish brown, narrowly cylindrical grains 1-1.5 mm long.

DISTRIBUTION. Shady turf, gardens, waste places, damp woods, thickets, and pastures throughout the state.

Nimblewill often forms dense stands because the lower, creeping parts of the stems easily root at the nodes and send up wiry, threadlike branches. In shady spots, it is an unwelcome lawn weed.

Nimblewill
Muhlenbergia schreberi

Glossary

Achene. A small, dry, 1-loculed, 1-seeded fruit that does not split open; the seed attaches to the fruit wall at one place.

Aerial roots. Roots originating above the ground or water.

Alternate. Not opposite, but borne at regular intervals at different levels, one per node.

Angular. Sharp-cornered.

Apex. Tip.

Appendage. A part secondary to something larger.

Ascending. Rising or curving upward.

Auricle. An earlobe-shaped or clawlike lobe or appendage.

Awl-shaped. Narrow and sharp-pointed; tapering upward from the base to a slender point.

Axil. The upper angle between a leaf or branch and the main axis.

Barbed. With spinelike hooks that are usually bent backward.

Basal. Pertaining to the base or foundation.

Beaked. Ending in a long, prominent point.

Berry. A pulpy fruit with immersed seeds and, typically, a thin skin; e.g., tomato.

Biennial. A plant that starts from seed in the spring or summer and produces a basal rosette of leaves the first year. The following spring the over-wintered plant sends up a shoot, which flowers, sets fruit, and dies in that season.

Bladdery. Inflated.

Blade. The expanded, flat part of a leaf or floral part.

Blunt. Dull, rounded.

Bract. A modified leaf.

Bristles. Stiff hairs or projections from a structure.

Bulb. An underground leaf bud with membranous or fleshy scales.

Bur. A seed or fruit bearing spines or prickles.

Calyx. The outer whorl of flower parts; usually green; it protects the petals in the bud.

Capsule. A dry dehiscent fruit composed of two or more carpels.

Carpel. A simple pistil, or one section of a compound pistil.
Cleft. Deeply cut or indented.
Conical. Resembling a cone.
Corolla. The inner whorl of the perianth; the collective name for petals.
Culm. A stem of a grass or sedge.
Deciduous. Falling away, as leaves at the end of the growing season; not persistent.
Decumbent. Reclining on the ground but with the tip ascending.
Dehiscent. Of a fruit, opening at maturity to release the seeds.
Dicot. Plants usually with net-veined leaves; the perianth parts usually number 4-5, and the vascular bundles are in a cylindrical arrangement in the stem.
Dioecious. With male and female flowers borne on separate plants.
Disk flowers. The tubular flowers in the Composite Family (Asteraceae).
Dissected. Divided into many segments.
Divided. Separated, or spreading widely.
Downy. Covered with soft, weak, short hairs.
Earmark. An identifying mark or feature; or a special characteristic.
Elliptic. Oval in outline with the widest part at or about the middle.
Elongate. *verb*: To become longer. *adj*.: Long and narrow, as certain leaves.
Entire. Smooth-edged, the margin without projections (teeth or lobes).
Floret. A small flower, usually one of a dense cluster.
Flower head. A dense cluster of stalkless or nearly stalkless flowers.
Follicle. A dry fruit of one carpel that opens down one side only.
Funnelform. Having the shape of a funnel.
Gland. A secreting surface or structure.
Glandular. Bearing glands or secreting organs.
Glossy. Smooth, shiny.
Halberd-shaped. Shaped like an arrowhead but with the basal lobes pointing outward at wide angles.
Herbaceous plant. A vascular plant that does not develop persistent woody tissue above ground.
Incised. Irregularly and deeply cut.
Indehiscent. Not splitting open at maturity.
Inflated. Puffed up.

Inflorescence. The flowering part of a plant, especially its arrangement.

Involucral bracts. A distinct whorl of small leaves subtending a flower or an inflorescence.

Lanceolate. Much longer than broad; widening above the base and tapering to the apex.

Legume. A dehiscent fruit of one carpel that typically opens along both upper and lower sides.

Ligule. A hairlike or membranous projection up from the inside of a grass sheath at its junction with the blade.

Linear. Long and narrow with the sides parallel.

Lobe. A rounded or pointed projection, larger than a tooth, from the margin of an organ.

Lobed. Bearing lobes.

Mealy. Flecked with another color, or covered with fine granules.

Membranous. Thin, papery, soft.

Monocarpic perennial. A plant that takes two or more years to flower and then dies.

Monocot. Plants usually with parallel-veined leaves, the perianth parts often in arrangements of 3 or 6, and the vascular bundles scattered in the stem.

Nerve. A vein or rib, as on some sepals.

Node. A place on a stem where one or more leaves arise; a knotlike enlargement.

Notched. Indented.

Noxious. Descriptive of a weed arbitrarily defined by law as being especially undesirable, troublesome, or difficult to control.

Nutlet. A small nut or nutlike fruit.

Oblanceolate. Narrow with the broadest part above the middle.

Oblong. With the sides nearly parallel most of their length.

Obovate. Broadest at the top and attached at the narrow end.

Ocrea. A membranous cylinder formed by the fusion of the two stipules at a node.

Opposite. Occurring two at the same level and on opposite sides of a stem.

Oval. Broadly elliptical.

Ovate. In shape like a long section of a hen's egg, with the broader end below the middle.

Ovoid. Oval in outline.

Palmate. Radiating from a point or center; may refer to leaves or veins.

Panicle. A much-branched cluster of flowers attached at the tips of the branches.

Pedicel.   The stalk of a single flower.

Peduncle.   A primary flower stalk, supporting either a solitary flower or a flower cluster.

Perennial.   A plant that lives for three or more years.

Perianth.   The floral envelope made up of the calyx and corolla, when present.

Persistent.   Remaining attached after like parts usually fall off.

Petal.   One of the inner perianth appendages of a flower, usually the colorful part of a flower.

Petiole.   The stalk of a leaf blade or of a compound leaf.

Pinnate.   A compound leaf with the leaflets on two opposite sides of an elongated axis.

Pistil.   The female or seed-bearing organ of a flower, consisting of the ovary, stigma, and style.

Pitted.   Marked with small depressions.

Pod.   A dry fruit that splits open.

Prickle.   A sharp-pointed projection growing from the surface of an organ.

Prostrate.   Lying on the ground.

Raceme.   A simple inflorescence with stalked flowers along a central stem.

Ray flower.   The strap-shaped or ligulate flower of the Composite Family (Asteraceae).

Recurved.   Curved backward.

Reflexed.   Bent backward.

Rhizome.   A more or less horizontal subterranean stem usually rooting at the nodes and becoming upcurved at the tip.

Ribbed.   With prominent ribs or grooves.

Rosette.   A cluster of leaves or other organs in a circular form, usually at ground level.

Scalloped.   Wavy.

Sepal.   One of the outer perianth appendages of a flower, usually green.

Sheath.   A tubular envelope, usually used for that part of a grass or sedge leaf that surrounds the stem.

Simple.   Of only one part, not divided or separated.

Sinus.   The space between two lobes.

Smooth.   Not rough.

Spatulate.   Spoon-shaped.

Spike.   A simple inflorescence with the flowers stalkless or nearly so, along a central stem.

Spikelet.   A floral unit, or cluster of a grass inflorescence made up of flowers and bracts.

Stalk.   The connecting or supporting part of an organ.

Stamen.   A male or pollen-producing organ of a flower.

Stigma. The part of the pistil that receives the pollen.

Stipule. One of the paired appendages at the base of certain leaves.

Stolon. An aboveground stem that lies on the ground and roots at the nodes.

Striate. Marked with streaks.

Style. The usually stalklike part of a pistil between the ovary and the stigma.

Subtending. Located beneath, often enclosing or embracing.

Succulent. Fleshy, juicy.

Summer annual. A plant that starts from seed in the spring and dies in the same year.

Taproot. A root system with a main root and smaller lateral roots.

Terminal. At the tip or apex.

Toothed. Bearing sawtoothlike projections along the margin.

Tubercle. A small, tuberlike body.

Tuft. A cluster or clump of hairs.

Umbel. An inflorescence in which the peduncles or pedicels of a cluster spring from the same place, like ribs of an umbrella.

Unisexual. Of one sex only, either all male or all female.

Utricle. A small, bladdery, 1-seeded fruit.

Waste place. An abandoned, neglected, or disturbed site.

Webbed. Covered with something woven or entangled.

Whorled. Of leaves or other parts, in groups of 3 or more, equally spaced at the same level around the stem.

Winged. Having a flat, membranous structure growing from the side or end of an organ.

Winter annual. A plant that starts from seed in autumn, develops a rosette of basal leaves before winter, and then flowers and sets seed the following spring or summer.

Bibliography

Bare, Janet E. 1979. *Wildflowers and Weeds of Kansas*. Lawrence: Regents Press of Kansas.

Barret, S.C.H., and B.F. Wilson. 1981. Colonizing ability in the *Echinochloa crus-galli* complex (barnyard grass). I. Variation in life history. *Can. J. Bot*. 59:1844-60.

Bassett, I.J., and C.W. Crompton. 1978. The biology of Canadian weeds, 32. *Chenopodium album. Can. J. Plant Sci*. 58:1061-72.

Bassett, I.J., and C.W. Crompton. 1982. The biology of Canadian weeds, 55. *Ambrosia trifida* L. *Can. J. Plant Sci*. 62:1003-10.

Bassett, I.J., and D.B. Munro. 1985. The biology of Canadian weeds, 76. *Solanum ptycanthum* Dun., *S. nigrum* L., and *S. sarrachoides* Sendt. *Can. J. Plant Sci*. 65:401-14.

Behrendt, S., and M. Hanf. 1979. *Grass Weeds in World Agriculture*. Ludwigshafen: BASF Aktiengesellschaft.

Best, K.F., and G.I. McIntyre. 1975. The biology of Canadian weeds, 9. *Thlaspi arvense* L. *Can. J. Plant Sci*. 55:279-92.

Bhowmik, P. C., and J.D. Bandeen. 1976. The biology of Canadian weeds, 19. *Asclepias syriaca* L. *Can. J. Plant Sci*. 56: 579-89.

Bianchini, F., and F. Corbetta. 1977. *Health Plants of the World*. New York: Newsweek Books.

Bush, P.S. 1977. *Wildflowers and the Stories Behind Their Names*. New York: Scribner's.

Chandler, J.M., and C.R. Oliver. 1979. *Spurred anoda: A potential weed in southern crops*. U.S. Department of Agricultural Science and Education Administration. Agriculture Reviews and Manuals, ARM S-2.

Culpeper, N. 1817. *The Complete Herbal*. London: Richard Evans.

Dalton, P.A. 1979. *Wildflowers of the Northeast in the Audubon Fairchild Garden*. Canaan, NH: Phoenix Pub.

Elmore, C.D., and S. McDaniel. 1986. Identification and distribution of the weedy spurges in the delta of Mississippi. *Weed Sci*. 34:911-15.

Fernald, M.L. 1970. *Gray's Manual of Botany*, 8th ed. New York: Van Nostrand.

Folkard, R. 1892. *Plant Lore, Legends, and Lyrics.* London: Sampson Low, Marston.

Frost, R.A., and P.B. Cavers. 1975. The ecology of pigweeds (*Amaranthus*) in Ontaria. I. Interspecific and intraspecific variation in seed germination among local collections of *A. powellii* and *A. retroflexus. Can. J. Bot.* 53:1276-84.

Gaertner, E.E. 1979. The history and use of milkweed (*Asclepias syriaca* L.) *Econ. Bot.* 33.

Garman, H. 1914. *Some Kentucky Weeds and Poisonous Plants.* Kentucky Agricultural Experiment Station Bulletin, No. 183. Lexington: State Univ. Press.

Gould, F.M.A., and D. Fairbrothers. 1972. A revision of *Echinochloa* in the United States. *Am. Mid. Nat.* 87:36-59.

Gross, R.S., P.A. Werner, and W.R. Hawthorn. 1980. The biology of Canadian weeds. 38. *Arctium minus* (Hill.) Bernh. and *Arctium lappa* L. *Can. J. Plant Sci.* 60:621-34.

Harris, B.C. 1972. *The Compleat Herbal.* Barre, MA: Barre.

Hatfield, A.W. 1971. *How to Enjoy Your Weeds.* New York: Sterling.

Haughton, C.S. 1978. *Green Immigrants.* New York: HarBrace J.

Herron, J.W., J.R. Martin, and A.J. Powell, Jr. Weeds of Kentucky Turf. Agr. 12. Lexington: University of Kentucky College of Agriculture, Cooperative Extension Service.

Hitchcock, A.S. 1950. *Manual of the Grasses of the United States.* Washington, D.C.: U.S. Government Printing Office.

Kindscher, K. 1987. *Edible Wild Plants of the Prairie: An Ethnobotanical Guide.* Lawrence: Univ. Press of Kansas.

Kingsbury, J.M. 1964. *Poisonous Plants of the United States and Canada.* Englewood Cliffs, NJ: P-H.

Lawrence, G.H.M. 1951. *Taxonomy of Vascular Plants.* New York: Macmillan.

Meijer, W. 1972. Composite Family (Asteraceae) in Kentucky. Lexington: University of Kentucky.

Meyer, J.E. 1981. *The Herbalist.* Glenwood, IL: Meyerbrooks.

Millspaugh, C.F. 1887. *American Medical Plants: An Illustrated and Descriptive Guide to the American Plants Used As Homeopathic Remedies.* New York: Boerick & Fafel.

Moerman, D.E. 1982. *Geraniums for the Iroquois.* Algonac, MI: Ref Pubns.

Monaghan, N. 1979. The biology of johnsongrass (*Sorghum halepense*). *Wes. Res.* 19:261-67.

Moore, R.J., and C. Frankton. 1974. *The Thistles of Canada.* Research Branch, Canada Department of Agriculture, Monograph #10.

Moore, R.J. 1975. The biology of Canadian weeds, 13. *Circium arvense* (L.) Scop. *Can. J. Plant Sci.* 55:1033-48.

Morton, J.F. 1981. *Atlas of Medicinal Plants of Middle America: Bahamas to Yucatan.* Springfield, IL: C.C. Thomas.

Muenscher, W.C. 1955. *Weeds.* 2d ed. New York: Macmillan.

Nebraska Weeds. 1975. Lincoln: Nebraska Department of Agriculture, State Capitol.

Richardson, J. 1981. *Wild Edible Plants of New England: A Field Guide.* Yarmouth, ME: DeLorme.

Robertson, K. 1981. The genera of Amaranthaceae in southeastern United States. *J. of Arn. Arb.* 62:267-314.

Rollins, R. 1981. Weeds of the Cruciferae (Brassicaceae) in North America. *J. of Arn. Arb.* 62:517-40.

Sauer, J.D. 1950. The grain amaranths: A survey of their history and classification. *Ann. Mo. Bot. Gard.* 37:561-632.

Scott, M., ed. 1986. *An Irish Herbal.* Wellingborough, Northamptonshire: Aquarian P.

Scriber, M.M., and C.R. Oliver. 1971. Two varieties of *Setaria viridis. Weed Sci.* 18:424-27.

Skinner, C.M. 1911. *Myths and Legends of Flowers, Trees, Fruits, and Plants.* Philadelphia: Lippincott.

Spencer, E.R. 1940. *Just Weeds.* New York: Scribner's.

Stary, F. 1983. *Poisonous Plants.* Prague: Hamlyn, Artia.

Step, E. 1926. *Herbs of Healing: A Book of British Simples.* London: Hutchinson.

Stucky, J.M., T.J. Monaco, and A.D. Worsham. 1980. *Identifying Seedling and Mature Weeds Common in the Southeastern United States.* Raleigh: North Carolina Agricultural Research Service and North Carolina Agricultural Extension Service, North Carolina State University.

Tull, D. 1987. *A Practical Guide to Edible and Useful Plants.* Austin: Texas Month Pr.

U.S. Department of Agriculture. 1971. *Common Weeds of the United States.* New York: Dover.

Vance, F.R., J.R. Jowsey, and J.S. McLean. 1977. *Wildflowers across the Prairies.* Saskatoon, Saskatchewan: Western Producer Prairie Books.

Vogel, V.J. 1970. *American Indian Medicine.* Norman: Univ. Of Oklahoma Press.

Voss, J., and V.S. Eifert. 1978. *Illinois Wild Flowers.* Popular Science Series Vol. III. Springfield: Ill. St. Museum.

Warwick, S.I., and L. Black. 1982. The biology of Canadian weeds, 52. *Achillea millefolium* L. *Can. J. Plant Sci.* 62:162-82.

Wax, L.M. 1979. Observations on the weedy amaranths. *Proc. N. Central Weed Control Conference,* vol. 34.

Wax, L.M., R.S. Fawcett, and D. Isely. 1981. *Weeds of the North Central States.* North Central Regional Research Publication

#281. Bulletin 772. University of Illinois at Urbana-Champaign, College of Agriculture, Agriculture Experiment Station.

Weaver, S.E., and E.L. McWilliams. 1980. The biology of Canadian weeds. *Amaranthus retroflexus* L., *A. powellii* S. Wats, and *A. hybridus* L. *Can. J. Plant Sci.* 60:1215-34.

Weaver, S.E., and W.R. Riley. 1982. The biology of Canadian weeds, 53. *Convolvulus arvensis* L. *Can. J. Plant Sci.* 62:461-72.

Weiner, M.A. 1972. *Earth Medicine—Earth Foods.* New York: Macmillan.

Werner, P.A., and R. Rious. 1977. The biology of Canadian weeds, 24. *Agropyron repens* (L.) Beauv. *Can. J. Plant Sci.* 57:905-19.

Wharton, M.E., and R.W. Barbour. 1971. *Wildflowers and Ferns of Kentucky.* Lexington: Univ. Press of Kentucky.

Wodehouse, R. 1945. *Hayfever Plants.* Waltham, MA: Chronica Botanica.

Woodward, C.J., and H.W. Rickett. 1979. *Common Wild Flowers of the Northeastern United States.* Woodbury, NY: Barron's.

Index of Common Names

Index of Scientific Names

*Synonym

Notes

Notes

Notes

Notes

Notes

Notes